Sponsored by the
Martinez Area Chamber of
Commerce & Tourist Bureau
Donated on Behalf of:

The UPS Store

Lou Schoeneman, Executive Director

Jerry & Marie Knutson
Dated: February 9, 2006

THE
BOX
BOOK

THE
BOX
BOOK

Original projects for all ages

Clare Beaton

Trafalgar Square Publishing

For Margaret

First published in the United States of America in 1997
by Trafalgar Square Publishing, North Pomfret, Vermont 05053

Printed and bound in Spain by Bookprint

Copyright © Collins & Brown Limited 1996

Text copyright Clare Beaton 1996

1 3 5 7 9 8 6 4 2

ISBN 1-57076-077-2
Library of Congress Catalog Card Number: 96-61022

Conceived, edited and designed by Collins & Brown Limited

Project Editor: Susan Martineau
Editor: Katie Bent
Art Director: Roger Bristow
Senior Art Editor: Ruth Hope
Photography: Geoff Dann
Designed by: Claire Graham
Cover design: Ruth Hope

Reproduction by J Film, Singapore

CONTENTS

COLLAGE AND PAINT

STRING AND THINGS

SHAPING BOXES

SECRET BOXES

INTRODUCTION

I N ITS ORIGINAL SENSE the word 'box' meant a container made of boxwood. It was generally used for storage and transportation. Traditionally, a box was a lasting and valuable object. Today, however, most boxes are disposable items made of cardboard or plastic.

Almost everything we buy is wrapped in packaging and many products come in boxes. We throw away masses of this packaging after a trip to the supermarket, however, if you make and decorate your own boxes you can recycle much of this wasted material.

As well as the boxes themselves, it is a good idea to keep anything else that could be useful – foil, card and decorative paper, for example, so that when you do have time and the creative urge you can start straight away! Most of the boxes in this book cost nothing to make. You just need time and a little imagination.

A decorated box makes a lovely gift on its own or with something

BELOW: *A quick and easy method of decorating boxes is to cover them with newspaper.*

ABOVE AND BELOW LEFT: *There are many different ways of making your box look attractive. These small wooden birds are part of the colourful decorations on the Indian Box on page 40.*

LEFT: *This square box is decorated in a collage of brightly coloured papers.*

special inside it. Some of the boxes in the book are designed with this in mind and give ideas on how they can reflect their contents.

The book is divided into four sections starting with the easier projects and progressing to more complicated ones. Nothing, however, is difficult and everything is explained with step-by-step instructions and clear illustrations. Techniques, such as stencilling and making papier mâché pulp, are fully described, as are various ways of preparing your box before you begin. All the templates used in the projects are given at the end of the book.

The first two chapters use everything from stencils and paints to shells and broken crockery to decorate ready-made boxes. The third chapter explains how to make your own special shaped boxes from paper, card or cardboard – like an oval Shaker box or a sparkly star-shaped one. The final chapter goes beyond what we might think of as a conventional box and creates wonderful objects that no one would realize were boxes at all!

BELOW: *Patterns and motifs on items you have around the house, like this African brooch and ceramic tile, can be a great source of inspiration.*

ABOVE: *Picture postcards can be used for simple découpage, as shown on page 25.*

BELOW: *This secret box in the shape of a hat is covered with gingham and home-made flowers.*

TOOLS AND EQUIPMENT

Fine paintbrush

Medium paintbrush

Large paintbrush

Y OU WILL PROBABLY already have most of the things listed here. However, there are one or two more specialist items you might need, such as a scalpel or craft knife.

CARDBOARD AND PAPER

Recycle card or cardboard packaging, as well as magazines, wrapping paper, maps, wallpaper and newspaper. Large boxes made of corrugated cardboard are strong and easy to cut. Flexible ridged cardboard (often used for packing bottles) is useful for shaping boxes.

GLUE

White household glue is useful, diluted, for making papier mâché and for mixing with grouting for fixing heavy objects. Copydex adhesive is suitable for gluing everything, including fabric.

PAINTS

Gouache paints or poster paints have the best covering power, and acrylics also work well. For

Coloured sewing thread

Assorted poster paints

Tracing paper

Fine sandpaper

Coarse sandpaper

Needles

Plastic ruler   Metal ruler

Scalpel

Scissors

Acrylic paint

Acrylic paint

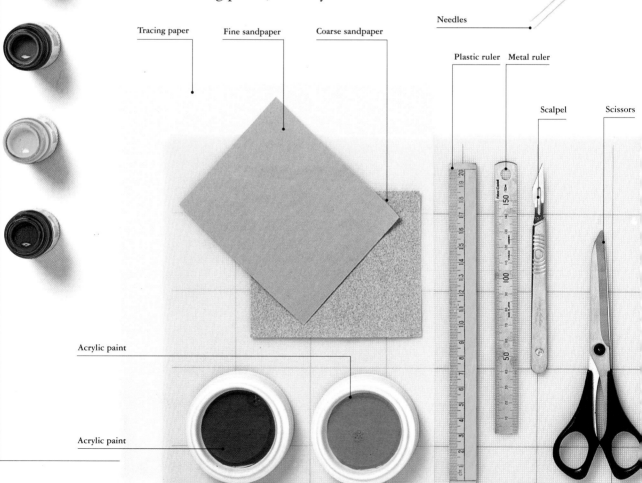

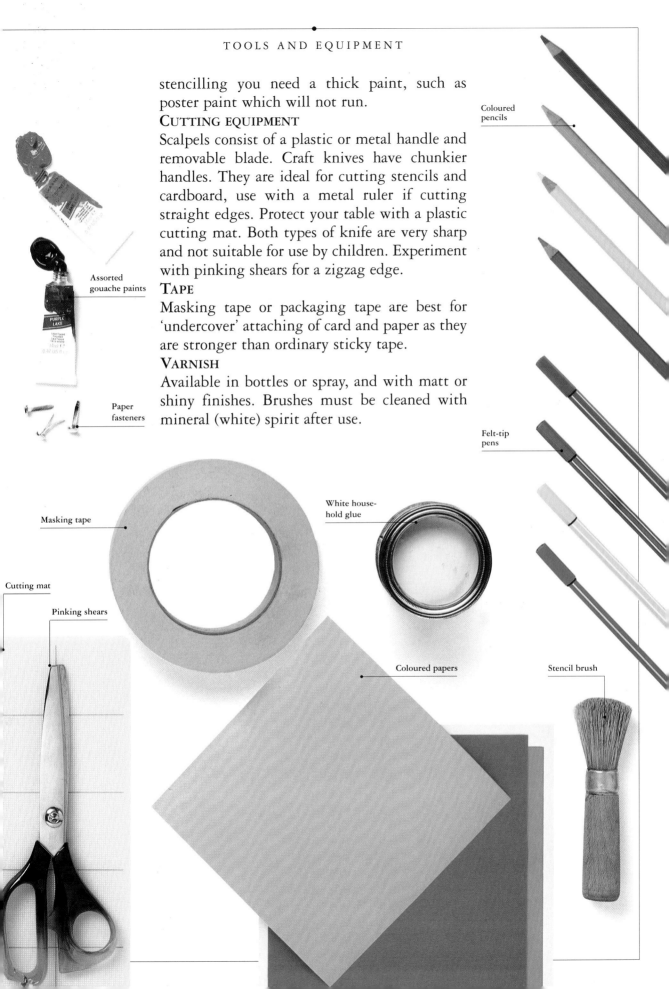

stencilling you need a thick paint, such as poster paint which will not run.

CUTTING EQUIPMENT

Scalpels consist of a plastic or metal handle and removable blade. Craft knives have chunkier handles. They are ideal for cutting stencils and cardboard, use with a metal ruler if cutting straight edges. Protect your table with a plastic cutting mat. Both types of knife are very sharp and not suitable for use by children. Experiment with pinking shears for a zigzag edge.

TAPE

Masking tape or packaging tape are best for 'undercover' attaching of card and paper as they are stronger than ordinary sticky tape.

VARNISH

Available in bottles or spray, and with matt or shiny finishes. Brushes must be cleaned with mineral (white) spirit after use.

Coloured pencils

Assorted gouache paints

Paper fasteners

Felt-tip pens

Masking tape

White house-hold glue

Cutting mat

Pinking shears

Coloured papers

Stencil brush

PREPARING YOUR BOX

EARLY ALL OF THE BOXES in this book are created using the ready-made boxes we find in our shopping. Packages for teabags, light bulbs, cookies, cereals and many other products, for instance, all make useful basic containers to start from. If you have the storage space, it's a good idea to build up and keep a selection of boxes so that you have some handy when you come to create a box, or if there's a special occasion requiring a decorated container. Even boxes which at first glance appear unsuitable can be easily adapted and strengthened by following the instructions shown here.

TYPES OF BOX

Chocolate Boxes With their many interesting shapes, lids and exotic finishes inside and out, they can be transformed into unusual boxes.

Shoe Boxes These make ideal bases with their stout card sides and removable lids.

Cheese Boxes Circular and semi-circular cheese boxes are particularly useful too, so never throw them away!

Cereal Packages As they are made from flexible cardboard which is useful for shaping into different styles of box, such as the Hat Box on page 84 or the Shaker Box on page 52.

Wooden Boxes Their surfaces need to be smoothed with fine sandpaper. Then they can be painted white and sanded again until the surfaces are silky.

Plastic Boxes Covered these boxes in a layer of glued newspaper pieces before being decorating.

INSIDES OF BOXES

If plain, these can simply be left as they are. If you have lined a box in strengthening newspaper pieces (see below) it can look attractive just like that (see the Fish Box on page 56). Instead of plain newspaper you could also try using comics, magazines or coloured newspaper pieces.

Alternatively you can paint the insides of your box in a colour to complement the exterior decoration or line them with patterned papers or fabric. If the box is a gift, or if you are making it to mark a special occasion, you could glue a message on to the inside of the lid.

CONTENTS OF BOXES

What you plan to keep or give in the box can be influential here too. A box filled with home-made chocolates or candies could be lined with

• STRENGTHENING A BOX •

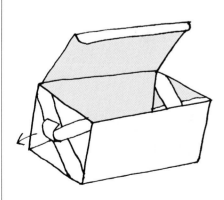

1 *Use masking tape to tape over any joins or flaps. This will give a flat surface on which to work.*

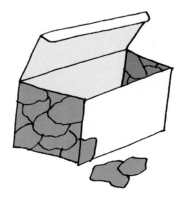

2 *Then cover the entire box, inside and out, with pieces of glued, torn newspaper. You may need 2 or 3 layers.*

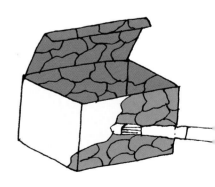

3 *Continue until the inside and outside of the box is covered and the box is firm and strong. Leave it to dry and then paint white.*

gold or silver doilies and if you leave the ends of the lining paper longer than the sides of the box you can fold them over on top of the contents. You could use gingham fabric or coloured paper in the same way to line a box of home-made cookies (see below).

LIDS

These can be made or adapted to wherever you want them. If you would like to change the position of an existing lid to suit the design of your box, you could move it from the side of a box, for example, to the top or vice versa, following the instructions below.

BOTTOMS OF BOXES

These should not be forgotten! You can either cover the underneath of your box in fabric or paper to match the sides and lid, or paint it to match the insides.

• MOVING A LID •

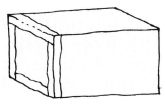

1 Using masking tape, tape down the unwanted opening.

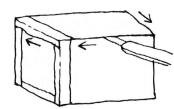

2 With a scalpel or craft knife, carefully cut a new lid along the corners of the box on 3 sides.

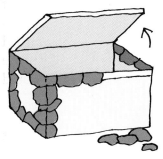

3 Tape along the cut edges with masking tape and then cover them with pieces of torn and glued newspaper. Cover the edges of the old lid too.

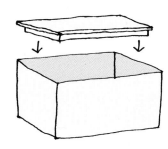

4 To make a removable lid, cut off the box top and glue a smaller piece of thick card on the inside. (See the Skyscraper Box on page 70.) If necessary, tape and cover the lid edges as before.

• LINING A BOX •

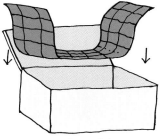
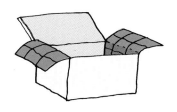
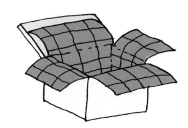

1 Cut your chosen fabric or paper into a strip the same width as the box and longer than the combined measurements of the bottom and short sides. Glue in position inside the box.

2 Cut a second piece of fabric or paper 'crossing' the first, making the flaps the same length as on the first piece. Glue inside the box. (If flaps are not required, then simply cut the fabric or paper flush with the edges of the box.)

3 Cut and glue a piece of fabric or paper on to the inside of the lid. The edges should be cut flush with the edges of the lid. Then fold the flaps over the contents of the box.

BASIC TECHNIQUES

YOU DON'T NEED ANY SPECIAL skills to create your own fabulous decorated box. However, you may find some of the basic techniques shown below come in handy.

PAPIER MÂCHÉ

Papier mâché pulp is used to mould shapes and create low relief, and also to add details and fill in gaps on sculptural pieces. The pulp is made from old newspapers and glue. You can make a flour and water paste with 2 heaped tablespoons of white flour mixed to a smooth consistency with 100ml/3½floz of water. Wallpaper paste can also be used (make it a little thicker than the instructions state). White household glue, diluted with water before use, is excellent and can be obtained from craft or art shops.

Simply make up a pulp, as shown below, building up layers on your box to the required shape or strength.

STENCILLING

It is best to use stencil paper (available from craft or art shops) for cutting stencils, although you can use thin card instead. Trace the shape required on to the stencil paper using the same technique as for tracing a template (see below). Then cut it out carefully with a scalpel or craft knife. When cutting, protect your surface with a cutting mat or similar.

Tape the stencil in position on your box and paint with a stiff stencil brush and thick paint. Remove the tape when the paint is dry and carefully lift off the stencil.

• PAPIER MÂCHÉ PULP •

1 *Tear newspaper into stamp-sized pieces and put them into a bowl. Cover with warm water and leave to soak overnight.*

2 *Squeeze the water out of the paper. Add some glue and mix thoroughly into a mush.*

• USING A TEMPLATE •

1 *Trace the template shape on to tracing paper, using a soft pencil.*

2 *Turn the tracing paper over and scribble over the pencil outline in soft pencil.*

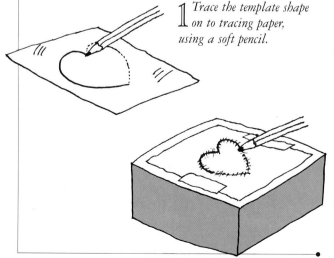

3 *Turn the tracing over again, tape it in position and retrace the line, pressing down firmly to give a solid outline.*

TEMPLATES

The templates at the end of the book will help you create the decorative boxes. You can also combine some of them to make different designs. If you use a template for cutting out fabric, simply pin the tracing (after Step 1) on to the fabric and cut through the tracing paper and fabric together.

CUTTING AND TEARING

There are many ways of cutting out images for gluing on to your box. For example, you can cut close around the image, leave a little background paper, or use pinking shears. Tearing gives a ragged edge.

VARNISHING

A coat or two of matt or shiny varnish will help to preserve your box and make it easier to keep clean. Always allow one coat to dry before applying another.

STITCHING

Stitching is very decorative and coloured yarn looks great on contrasting fabrics or even card. Use different stitches to construct your box, sewing along the edges to join pieces of card.

TEA-DYEING FABRIC

Dyeing fabric in tea creates an attractive antique effect and is especially effective on white or light-coloured fabrics. Make a strongish pot of tea and pour it all over the fabric, making sure it is completely covered. Leave to soak for about three hours, then hang up to dry.

SCORING

Before folding card it helps to score it. Position a ruler (preferably metal) along the line you wish to fold and draw a scalpel or craft knife lightly across the card against the ruler. The scored side is the side that will be showing when the box is finished.

• CUTTING AND TEARING •

Cut closely with scissors

A zig-zag border cut with pinking shears

Ragged edge torn by hand

A border cut roughly with scissors

Torn coloured paper leaves a white edge

• STITCHING •

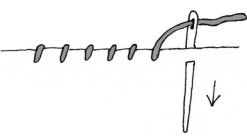

Overstitch
This stitch is useful for neatening raw fabric edges and for joining pieces of card. Work from left to right with evenly spaced stitches as shown.

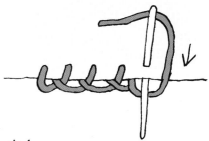

Blanket stitch
Work from left to right. Bring yarn through from the back and go in again a suitable distance away. Hold edge with thumb and forefinger and with the needle in a verticle position pull it down through the loop of yarn. Continue with the next stitch.

COLLAGE AND PAINT

Here are fourteen ideas for decorating boxes – all painted or covered in coloured papers. There are stencil designs and mosaics created from cut and torn paper. All the templates needed are given at the back of the book. The designs use ready-made boxes from everyday shopping as their base and, although they are the easiest boxes in the book, they are just as attractive as the more elaborate ones which come later.

TEA-TIME BOX

This box would make a lovely present filled with
herbal or fruit teabags. The details, such as the spots on
the teapot, are added at the end. You could either paint them
freehand using a stencil brush or print them using a
potato block or similar.

SHOPPING LIST

Purple paint

•

Wooden box

•

Fine sandpaper

•

Tracing paper

•

Masking tape

•

Stencil paper and brush

•

Scalpel or craft knife

•

Thick paint for stencilling

•

Varnish

• WHAT TO DO •

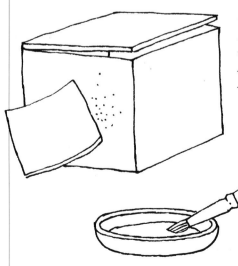

1 *Paint the box purple
and sand it smooth
when dry. Apply a
second coat of paint and
sand again when dry.*

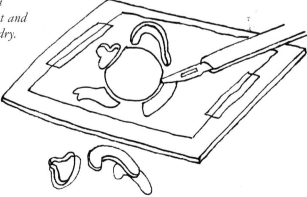

2 *Trace the teapot stencil shapes from the templates
on page 89 and tape on to the stencil paper. Cut
out with the scalpel or craft knife.*

3 *Tape the stencil on the box with masking tape, making sure that it is positioned centrally.*

THREAD REEL BOX

Here a shallow cardboard container makes an ideal storage unit for sewing thread. A small repeated image forms a very effective reflection of the contents of the box. The template for the thread reels is shown on page 89. After stencilling the pattern on to the box, you simply need to paint on the loose threads freehand using a fine paintbrush.

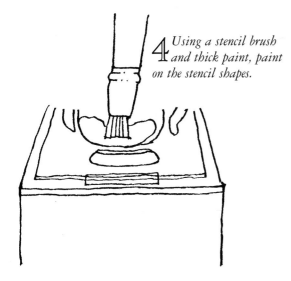

4 *Using a stencil brush and thick paint, paint on the stencil shapes.*

5 *Allow the box to dry thoroughly before carefully removing the stencil.*

6 *Continue stencilling the sides of the box with the teacup and cake stencils. Leave each stencil to dry before doing another. Finish with a leaf stencil in each corner of the lid and any other decoration of your choice. Then varnish.*

MARBLED PAPER BOX

It's simple to create a gift box using decorative wrapping paper and whatever size box you require. For a coordinated effect colour the inside of the box to match the paper.

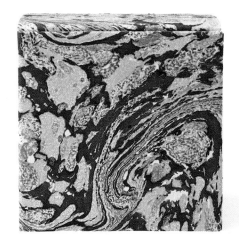

SHOPPING LIST

Box
•
Paint of your choice
•
Decorative paper
•
Glue

RIGHT: *A huge variety of decorative papers is available from specialist art, craft and stationery shops or you can use ordinary gift-wrap.*

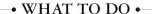

• WHAT TO DO •

1 *Paint the inside and bottom of the box in a colour of your choice. Leave it to dry.*

2 *Cut a strip of decorative paper 3cm/1¼in wider than the box and long enough to go around the 4 sides including a 1cm/⅜in overlap. It can be torn, cut straight or trimmed with pinking shears.*

3 *Place the box on its side and glue the paper around it with the join at the back and an equal overlap top and bottom.*

4 *Cut the overlap carefully at each of the 8 corners. Starting at the bottom, fold and glue the overlaps down. Press them firmly to stick well.*

5 *Stand the box on its bottom and fold and glue the overlaps inside, pressing them until stuck. Glue the fourth side up over the lid.*

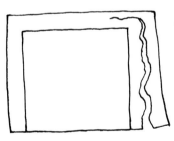

6 *Cut a piece of paper to fit the lid with a 1.5cm/⅝in overlap on 3 sides. Leave one edge straight. Tear, cut straight or trim the other 3 sides with pinking shears to match the other piece of paper.*

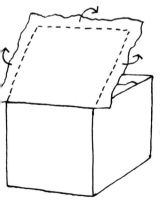

7 *Placing the straight edge flush with the hinged edge of the lid, glue the paper down. Cut the overlaps at the corners and fold and glue down under the lid, pressing firmly.*

MAP BOX

Start by choosing a box large enough to hold a collection of maps. Then cover it in the same way as the marbled paper box, this time using old maps you no longer need. If you are making the box as a gift you could use maps of someone's favourite holiday destination or local area.

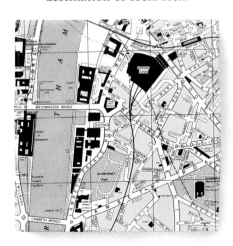

BIRD BOX

An old wooden cigar box is ideal for this project. Once the
lid design is complete, you can decorate the sides of the box in
a repeat pattern of small images using brightly coloured paints.
Here a fir tree design is used for the sides of the box and
a sun design for the sides of the lid.

SHOPPING LIST

Wooden box
•
White paint
•
Fine sandpaper
•
Tracing paper
•
Paints of your choice
•
Blue, red and yellow paint
•
Varnish

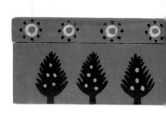

• WHAT TO DO •

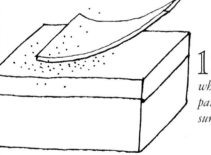

1 *Prepare the box
carefully. Paint it
white and sand the
paint to a smooth
surface when dry.*

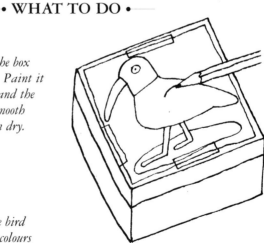

2 *Trace the bird
template on page
90 on to the lid,
taking care that it is
positioned centrally.*

3 *Paint the bird
with the colours
of your choice. Leave
each colour to dry
before applying
the next.*

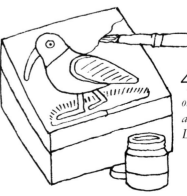

4 *Apply blue paint
to the background
on the lid, the lid sides
and the inside rim.
Leave to dry.*

LEFT: *Painting on wood is a very satisfying process. By using a small brush it is possible to include a great deal of detail.*

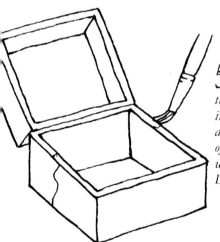

5 *Use red paint for the sides of the main box and its rim. When dry decorate the insides of the lid and box with yellow paint. Leave to dry.*

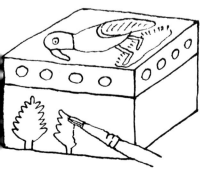

6 *Decorate the sides with repeat patterns and varnish when dry.*

LIZARD BOX

Use the lizard template on page 90 to create another attractive box in the same way as the bird box. Here bright primary shades are used for a really eye-catching effect. Other animal templates are given on pages 90–91.

To achieve a solid smooth finish, apply a second coat of paint to the template when the first is dry. Then you simply need to add the fine decorative details such as the speckled background by hand afterwards.

STAMP BOX

This eclectic collage is created from used postage
stamps. You can either collect them from your own mail
or buy bumper packs from junk shops. However, don't use
anything valuable! When sticking the stamps down take
care to glue the corners firmly in position.

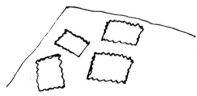

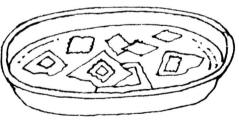

SHOPPING LIST

Stamps
•
Box
•
Glue
•
Varnish

• WHAT TO DO •

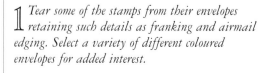

1 *Tear some of the stamps from their envelopes
retaining such details as franking and airmail
edging. Select a variety of different coloured
envelopes for added interest.*

2 *If you plan to use the stamps alone remove them from
their envelopes by placing them in cold water and
leaving for 10 minutes or so until the stamps float off
the paper. Dry out face down on newspaper.*

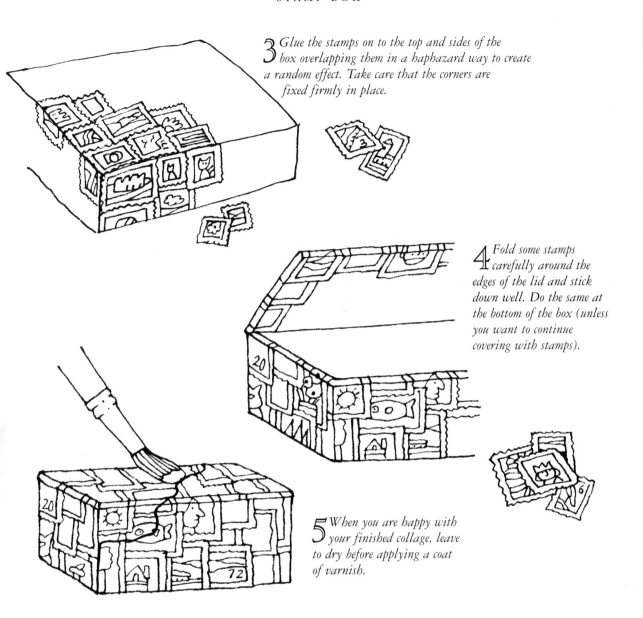

3 Glue the stamps on to the top and sides of the box overlapping them in a haphazard way to create a random effect. Take care that the corners are fixed firmly in place.

4 Fold some stamps carefully around the edges of the lid and stick down well. Do the same at the bottom of the box (unless you want to continue covering with stamps).

5 When you are happy with your finished collage, leave to dry before applying a coat of varnish.

SOCCER BOX

You can create an inexpensive but personal gift for a soccer fan by cutting out their favourite players from old sports magazines, postcards or photographs and gluing them to the top of an empty box or biscuit tin. Complete the effect by putting the colours of their team around the edge of the box — either in paint, ribbon or coloured paper.

You could use the same idea for different soccer teams, or other sports, such as rugby.

BLACK SHELL BOX

This very effective box is extremely simple to make.
Against a plain painted background cut-out images look very
clear and strong. You could also cut or tear motifs from magazines
or comics – choosing appropriate pictures if the box is a gift.

SHOPPING LIST

Box
•
Black paint
•
Shell design wrapping paper or similar
•
Glue
•
Varnish

• WHAT TO DO •

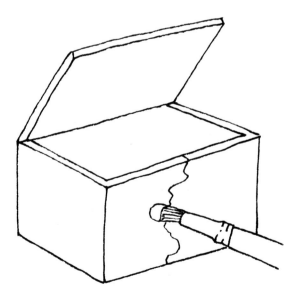

1 *When you have prepared your box, paint
the inside and outside with black paint.
Then leave it to dry.*

MEMORABILIA BOX

Make a holiday collection of plane, train and museum tickets, decorative food wrappers and restaurant bills as well as photographs and postcards. Cut and torn, then glued as a collage on the sides of a box, they make a lovely reminder of your trip. Finish with a label attached on top with a foreign postage stamp.

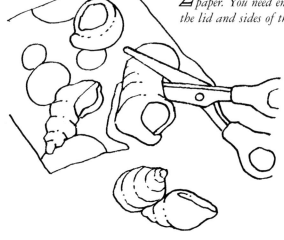

2 *Cut a selection of shells from the paper. You need enough to decorate the lid and sides of the box.*

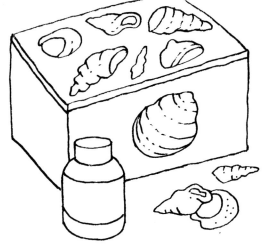

3 *Arrange the shell cut-outs on the lid and sides and then glue in position. Press down firmly with your fingertips.*

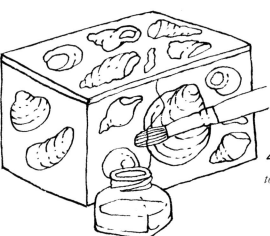

4 *When the cut-outs are dry, apply an even coat of varnish to all sides of the box.*

MOSAIC BOX

Cut out textured or plain coloured papers to create your
own mosaic-style box. Try stylized shapes, such as a butterfly
or fleurs-de-lis, or a series of geometric patterns to fit the
surfaces of the box. The background colour should
complement that of the paper.

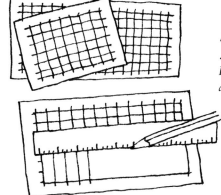

SHOPPING LIST

Box	Coloured pens
Paint of your choice for inside	Tracing paper
White paint	Magazines or coloured papers
Plain paper	Glue

• WHAT TO DO •

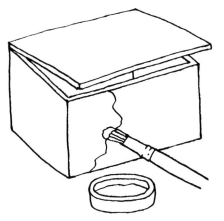

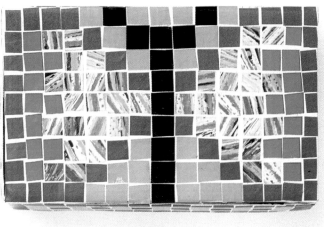

1 *Paint the inside of the box in the colour
of your choice and leave it to dry. Then
paint the outside white.*

2 *Measure the top
and sides of the box.
Divide the length and
depth of each into squares
of approximately
1.5cm/⅝in. Draw
out a grid on plain
paper for each surface.*

3 *Using coloured pens on tracing paper placed over the grids, work out the patterns and colours you want on the box.*

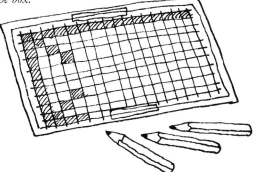

4 *Cut your magazines or coloured papers into 1.5cm/⅝in squares to match the colours of your tracing paper designs. Do not worry if the coloured squares are not exactly the same size or shape. Keep each colour in a separate pile.*

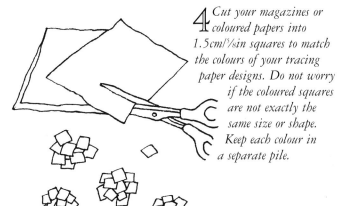

5 *Following your tracing paper design, glue the coloured paper pieces on to the box starting with the squares along the edges. Leave a tiny gap between each piece and press down firmly. Continue until the design is complete.*

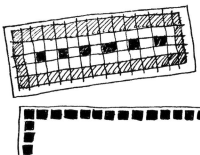

6 *Finish by decorating the sides in the same way using the tracing paper designs as a guide.*

PICTURE MOSAICS

You can create a mosaic by cutting up photographs, postcards, or other pictures into small squares and sticking them down well, leaving small gaps between the individual pieces. Choose pictures smaller than the area to be covered to allow for the gaps.

Cut up the picture, keeping the pieces in order for reassembly. Always glue down the corner and edge pieces first – rather like assembling a jigsaw – and then arrange the other pieces evenly in between.

TORN PAPER BOX

For this kind of more random mosaic it makes sense
to sketch your designs on to the box beforehand to use as a
rough guide when fixing on the paper pieces. You don't
need to follow the design precisely, but it does help
to have a rough layout from which you can work.

SHOPPING LIST

Box
•
Black paint
•
Tracing paper (optional)
•
Magazines or coloured papers
•
Glue

• WHAT TO DO •

*1 Paint the inside of the
box with black paint
and leave it to dry.*

*2 Measure the top and
sides of the box and
work out your design for
each. There are templates
to trace on page 91. Draw
or trace your design
on to the box.*

*3 Work out the colours you need
and tear up magazines or
coloured papers into small finger-
nail-sized pieces. Keep
each colour in a
separate pile.*

*4 Tear out large shapes
such as hearts and flower
stalks in one piece.*

LEFT: *In this freer version of the paper mosaic on pages 26–27, the decorative paper is torn rather than cut and then applied so that it overlaps.*

5 *Start gluing the paper pieces on to the box beginning with the background. Overlap the pieces and press down firmly.*

ANIMAL BOX

Draw a simple shape on the back of some patterned paper or use one of the templates on pages 90–91 as a guide. You could use a single image or several of the same shape. Then tear out your design and use it to decorate a painted box. Apply a layer of varnish for a durable finish.

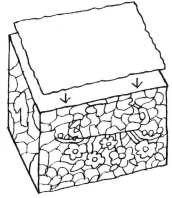

6 *When you have completed the top and sides, tear out one large piece of coloured paper to glue on to the bottom of the box.*

String and Things

All the boxes in this chapter, except
the lattice box, are decorated with small
things you can collect with a design
in mind – buttons, seeds, string, yarn,
broken china, shells and small toys. There
is no limit to what you can use. The basic
ideas and their variations are intended
to inspire you to make your own design
according to whatever bits and
bobs you have to hand.

Appliqué Letters Box

Fabrics look wonderful either glued flat on to boxes or softly padded. Try combining patterned fabrics together such as spots, stripes or floral. Dyeing the fabric in tea before use gives a marvellous antique look (see page 13).

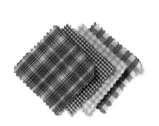

SHOPPING LIST

Box with fold-up lid

•

Beige paint

•

Enough small-checked brown cotton fabric to cover box

•

Fabric glue

•

3 small pieces of blue, red and yellow checked fabric

•

Beige and dark brown thread

•

Tracing paper

•

Wadding (batting) for cut-outs

•

Thin grey yarn

•

8 pearl buttons

•

Small piece of white cotton fabric

• WHAT TO DO •

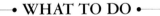

1 *Paint the inside beige. Cut a strip of brown fabric 3cm/1¼in wider than the depth of the box, to go around the 4 sides with an overlap of 1cm/⅜in. Cut a second piece to cover both sides of the lid plus 1cm/⅜in extra on all sides.*

2 *Glue the fabric on to the lid as shown, starting inside so that it is flush with the edge of the hinged lid. Glue the large strip around the box sides, with an equal overlap top and bottom, starting on the back. Glue the overlaps down.*

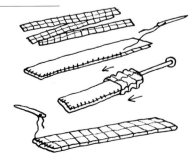

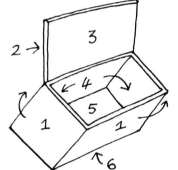

3 *Cut blue fabric into 4 strips 20cm/8in x 4.5cm/1¾in. Fold lengthways, checked sides together, and stitch the side and one end. Turn right side out. Sew ends; press flat.*

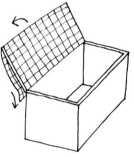

4 *Cut 3 hearts in re fabric using the template on page 92. Cut 3 slightly smaller hearts from wadding (batting). Joi the two layers overstitching in grey yarn (see page 13).*

LEFT: *If you are making the box as a present for someone then a lovely finishing touch is to stitch the recipient's name on the 'letter'.*

5 Cut out 2 yellow bird bodies and 2 blue wings using the templates on page 92. Attach the wings to bodies with a spot of glue so that each bird faces a different way. Cut 2 smaller bird shapes out of wadding (batting). Join the fabric and wadding (batting) with overstitching in grey yarn. Sew eyes in brown thread.

6 Cut 8 circles of yellow fabric about 3.5cm/1⅜in across and 8 smaller circles of wadding (batting). Join together with grey yarn, overstitching the sides. Sew pearl buttons on to the centres with beige thread.

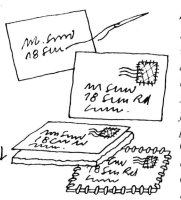

7 Cut a 7.5cm/3in x 10cm/4in rectangle of white fabric. Sew a name and address on it in dark brown thread. Cut a small stamp-sized shape of red fabric and overstitch in position with beige thread. Oversew franking lines in brown thread. Cut a piece of wadding (batting) for the letter and join together with yarn, overstitching the sides.

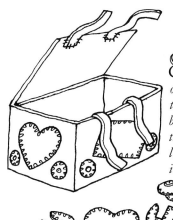

8 Glue the cut-out pieces in position on the top and sides of the box. Lastly glue 2 blue checked ties under the front edge of the lid and 2 to match inside the front.

Rooster Box

Any old scraps of yarn can be used to make this design except mohair which is too hairy! Rainbow or flecked yarn can be used to great effect here too. If you want to cover just part of the box surface, for example the sides, you will need to paint the box first.

SHOPPING LIST

Box large enough for template
on page 92

•

Tracing paper

•

Black felt-tip

•

Glue or double-sided tape

•

Coloured yarns

•

Small black bead

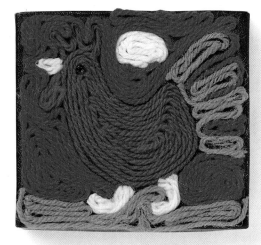

• WHAT TO DO •

1 *Trace the rooster design on to the lid of the box using the template on page 92, then go over the outline in black felt-tip.*

2 *If using double-sided tape, cover the lid with strips of it and remove the backing. When attaching yarn take care not to touch the surface or it will lose its stickiness. If using glue just apply to each area as you cover it with yarn.*

STRING BOX

Using the same technique you can create very effective designs with coloured string instead of yarn. The templates for this leaf and crown are given on pages 93–94 or you could use any of the other templates, such as the eggcup and teacup, at the back of the book. If you wish you could create a design of your own, perhaps using different images on each side of the box, which follow a similar scheme. Simply draw your designs on the sides of the box and fill in the areas with coloured string, as shown below.

3 *Start in the centre of the picture. Using generous lengths of yarn press the end of the yarn on to the sticky surface and fill in the various shapes with appropriate colours. Keep the yarn strands close together, covering the surface well.*

4 *Cut the end of the yarn as you finish filling each area and push down firmly.*

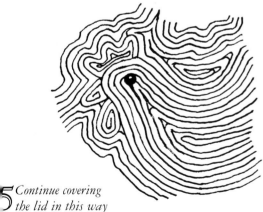

5 *Continue covering the lid in this way until finished. Then push a glued bead in position for the eye.*

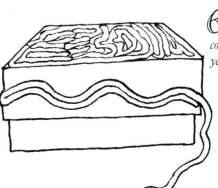

6 *Decorate the edges of the lid with a continuous 'wave' of yellow yarn.*

BUTTON BOX

This box was a ready-made heart-shaped one but
you could easily make your own. Simply trace off the heart
template on page 92 and follow the instructions given for
the fish and star-shaped boxes on pages 54–57.

SHOPPING LIST

Grouting

•

Glue

•

Plastic container with lid

•

Selection of buttons: mother of
pearl, plastic and brass

•

Box

•

Scrap of card

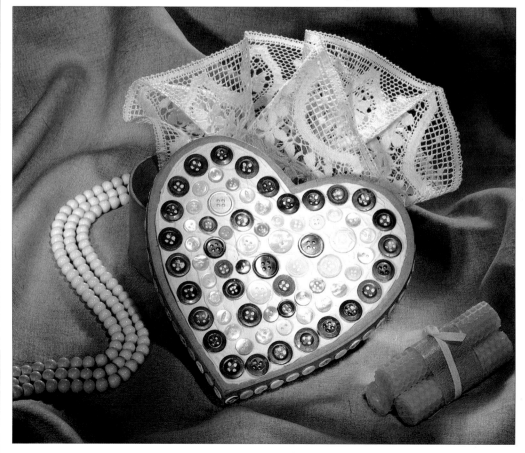

LEFT: *For a perfect
Valentine gift fill
the decorated box
with chocolates or
home-made heart-
shaped cookies.*

• WHAT TO DO •

1 Mix the grouting with glue and a little water to a thick smooth consistency. The glue will prevent cracking. Keep the mixture in a sealed container to prevent it from drying out.

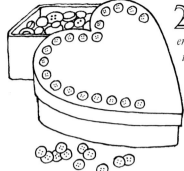

2 Sort out the buttons to make sure there are enough to cover the lid of the box. Put aside enough to make an edge of one kind of button.

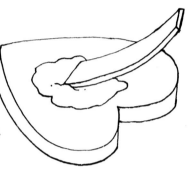

3 Cover the lid of the box with a thinnish layer of grouting mixture, smoothing it out with a scrap of card. Stop 5mm/¼in from the edge.

4 Stick a row of buttons around the edge, placing them carefully in position and pressing down well.

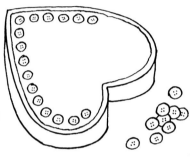

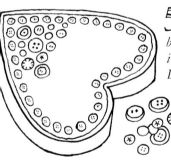

5 Fill in the rest of the lid with the remaining buttons laid close together in a random pattern. Leave to dry overnight. Any grouting left on the buttons can be scraped off carefully when dry.

CERAMIC BOX

Use the same technique to stick on any broken china you might have (or break a chipped or cracked piece by placing it in a plastic bag and dropping!), but apply the grouting more thickly to hold the broken china in place. Use tiny pieces to fill in gaps. Cover the lid first and the lid side the next day. You can paint the body of the box in a matching colour.

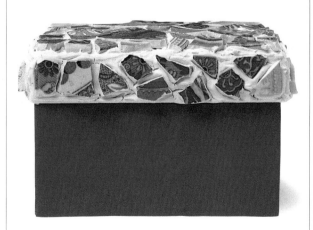

6 Apply a border of grouting around the side of the lid and stick on a row of similar-sized buttons. Leave to dry.

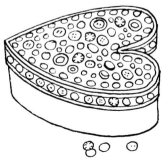

JEWELLED CASKET

The casket is decorated with brightly coloured foil wrappers from candies, cookies and cakes, and completed with the luxury of make-believe jewels! If you don't want to go to the expense of buying the jewels, you could remove a few beads from an old necklace.

SHOPPING LIST

Rectangular box with fold-up lid

Piece of thin card

Masking tape

Newspaper and glue

Pieces of gold and coloured foil
(e.g. candy wrappers)

Self-adhesive 'jewels' and beads

Tassel

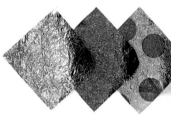

• WHAT TO DO •

1 *First make the roof-like lid of the casket. Cut out a piece of card the same size as the existing lid. Tape the card to the lid along its long edge so that it extends the lid.*

2 *Cut out 2 equilateral triangles of card with the sides the same length as the width of the box. Fold along the join in the extended lid to meet the front of the box and tape one triangle to each end of this new 'roof'.*

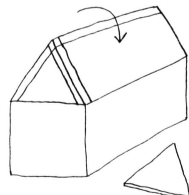

3 *Glue pieces of newspaper all over the box, inside and out, until the surface is smooth and firm. Leave to dry. Cover the inside and outside of the box completely with pieces of gold foil. These can overlap, but the sides of the box should be as smooth as possible.*

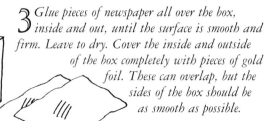

ABOVE: *A box that is as pretty as its contents of
beads, brooches and other trinkets.*

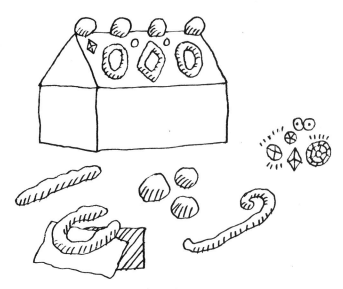

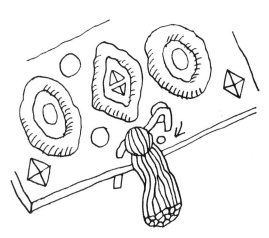

4 *Form some of the coloured foil into smooth strips
and others into balls. Position these carefully over
the box in a pattern of your choice. Decorate the box
further by sticking on 'jewels' and beads.*

5 *Make a small hole in the front of the lid. Cut
the loop of the tassel and push both ends through
to the inside. Securely tape down the loose threads
on the inside. Cover the tape with gold foil.*

INDIAN BOX

You can use all kinds of small figures, decorations and odds
and ends of fabric to create a real extravaganza of a box. Try doing
a seasonal one for Christmas using cake decorations, tinsel
and other sparkly ornaments like sequins.

SHOPPING LIST

Box

•

Paints of your choice

•

Small wooden figures and birds

•

Scalpel or craft knife

•

Glue

•

Coloured foil

•

Pinking shears

•

Self-adhesive jewels

•

Braid

•

Sequins

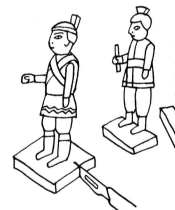

• WHAT TO DO •

1 *Paint the inside of the box and leave it to dry. Then paint the lid and sides a different colour. Leave to dry.*

2 *If the figures have little stands, carefully cut off the back part so the figures can be stuck flat on to the box. Stick evenly around the box so that the stands are flush with the bottom of the box.*

3 *Cut the coloured foil into different shapes, some with pinking shears, and stick between the figures. Add a few 'jewels'.*

4 *Glue a length of braid around the top of the box so that the bobbles hang between the figures. Glue sequins along the braid.*

ABOVE: *Make this box as extravagant as you like. The more elements you add the better it will look.*

5 *Glue the birds, facing each other, on to the centre of the lid.*

6 *Glue more foil shapes and stick more 'jewels' on to the top of the lid and around the birds to complete the effect.*

GOLD TOY BOX AND BEETLE BOX

To create the Gold Toy Box (right), cover the lid of a box with miniature 'cracker' toys, filling in the gaps with small beads and buttons. When the glue is dry and the toys firmly in place, spray it all over with an even coat of gold paint. To make the Beetle Box (left), cover a box in brightly coloured paper or paint and stick semi-circles of red paper cut with pinking shears over the corners. Then glue a selection of coloured plastic insects over the box.

FRUIT BOX

Corrugated cardboard is strong and very easy to cut – and most cardboard boxes are made out of this type of cardboard. You don't need to try and paint the sides of the cut cardboard here and you could also experiment with different-shaped cut-outs.

SHOPPING LIST

Box	Paints for cut-outs
Dark green paint	Thin black pen
Tracing paper	Glue
Corrugated cardboard	Varnish
Scalpel or craft knife	

• WHAT TO DO •

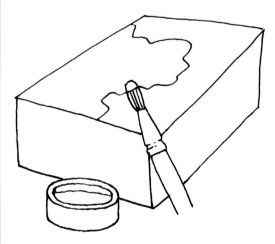

1 *Start by painting the sides and lid of the box dark green. Leave to dry before attempting to add the cut-out shapes.*

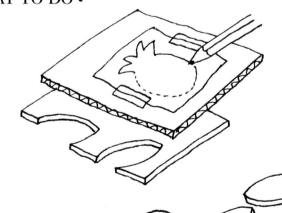

2 *Using the templates on page 94, trace and cut out enough cardboard cut-outs to make a decorative arrangement on the top and sides of the box.*

HOLLY BOX

Make a festive holly box in the same way, this time using the leaf template on page 94. Speckle dark green paint over the flat-painted leaves with an old toothbrush or stiff paintbrush to give a natural textured effect. When completely dry, glue coloured sequins on to the sides of the box between the cut-outs.

3 *Paint one side of the cut-outs in bright, flat colours. Some colours may need 2 coats to cover well. Leave them to dry.*

4 *Shade one side of the painted cut-outs with a stiff brush and darker thick paint. Add other details such as speckles to create texture.*

5 *When the cut-outs are dry, draw in any fine details such as leaf veins with a thin black pen.*

6 *Glue the cut-outs in position on the box and leave to dry before applying a coat of varnish.*

SEED BOX

All kinds of natural materials can make attractive
box coverings. Look out for seeds, dried seaweed, fir cones,
leaves, shells and anything else you might discover on country
and coastal walks. Leave them to dry before attaching them
to the surfaces of the box.

SHOPPING LIST

Box

•

Corrugated cardboard (enough to
cover lid and sides of box)

•

Glue

•

3 fir cones

•

Raffia

•

Pumpkin/melon seeds

• WHAT TO DO •

1 *Measure the 4 sides of
the box and cut pieces
of corrugated cardboard
to match. Glue them on
to the sides.*

2 *Measure the lid of
the box and cut a
piece of corrugated card-
board to fit. Cut 3 small
central holes for the fir
cones to sit in. Glue the
cardboard on to the lid.*

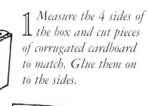

3 *Glue 3 pieces of raffia
evenly spaced along the
front and back sides of the
box. Glue one piece in the
centre of both ends.*

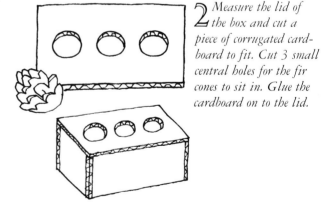

4 *Glue seeds around
the raffia 'stalks'
to create a series of
wheatear shapes.*

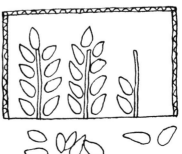

ABOVE: *This natural-looking box is very easy to make – you
don't even need to paint the sides of the box.*

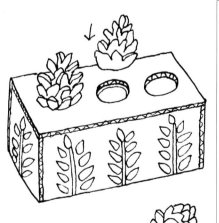

5 *Glue the 3 fir cones into
the holes on the lid and
leave the box to dry.*

SHELL BOX

Mix some grouting with glue as for the Button Box
on pages 36–37, adding a few drops of coloured ink if you
like. Use a wooden box to take the weight of the shells and
grouting and arrange your pattern of shells to be ready as soon
as the grouting is applied. Push the shells down into the
grouting, filling gaps with tiny shells. Make a border
with a shell necklace.

LATTICE BOX

Using coloured tissue paper to line the box and wrap
up anything you put in it creates a lovely effect as the tissue
will show through the lattice-work lid. This looks especially
effective if you use contrasting colours of paint
and tissue paper.

SHOPPING LIST

Shoe box with
removable lid

•

Tracing paper (optional)

•

Scalpel or craft knife

•

Black and yellow paint

•

Coloured tissue paper

BELOW: *You can combine
the 4 basic templates on
page 95 to create a myriad
of different patterns,
as here.*

• WHAT TO DO •

1 *Work out your design for the lattice lid
using shapes that work well together to create
a lacy effect when cut out. (See the 4 templates
on page 95 and the 3 designs above.)*

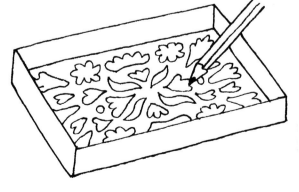

2 *Trace or draw the design on the inside of the lid.
The shapes should be quite close together but not
too close or the lid will disintegrate when cut.*

3 Cut out the shapes carefully using a scalpel or craft knife.

POT-POURRI BOX

A smaller version of the box shown opposite would make an ideal pot-pourri container. Keep the cut-out shapes as large as possible so that you can see as well as smell the pot-pourri. This particular design would make an inexpensive gift. It is made from an empty cardboard cheese box but other small, unusually-shaped boxes, such as chocolate boxes, would also be suitable.

4 Paint the inside and outside of the lid in black paint making sure that the edges of the lattice work are painted too.

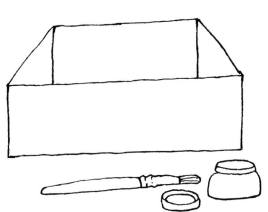

5 Paint the inside and outside of the rest of the box with yellow paint and leave it to dry overnight before filling.

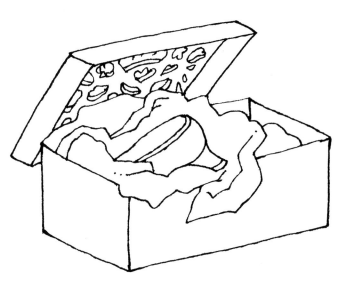

6 Line the lid and insides of the box with coloured tissue paper, also using it to wrap up the contents.

SHAPING
BOXES

*Although modern packaging offers
a variety of ready-made box shapes, here
are some special ones you can make yourself
and decorate with some of the ideas already
described. There are templates at the back
of the book to help you but you could invent
many more. It is especially pleasing if you
find a shape appropriate for a special gift
– the star on page 54 for a star-gazer
or the fish on page 56 for an angler!*

DICE BOX

This simple cube makes a useful box for wrapping an awkward-shaped gift. Wrap the item well in tissue paper and place it inside. You can change the size of the template on page 97 to make smaller or larger boxes.

SHOPPING LIST

Tracing paper

•

Stiff white paper

•

Scalpel or craft knife

•

Ruler

•

21 black self-adhesive spots

•

Double-sided tape

• WHAT TO DO •

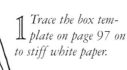

1 Trace the box template on page 97 on to stiff white paper.

2 Cut it out carefully using the scalpel or craft knife.

3 Using the scalpel or craft knife and the ruler, lightly score the box along the dotted lines.

4 Stick black dots on the sides in the same order as the dice.

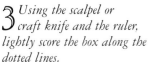

5 With the dotted side uppermost stick strips of double-sided tape on the 4 side flaps.

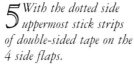

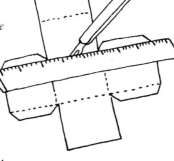

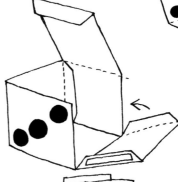

6 Fold gently along the scored lines to form the box. Remove the double-sided tape backing and carefully press the sides together.

DESK TIDY

This divided box made with cardboard tubes, is perfect for small items such as paper clips, thumbtacks and rubber bands. As an alternative to the stencilled design on the lid you could paint a small free-hand picture or stick on a cut-out.

SHOPPING LIST

7 cardboard tubes cut into 5cm/2in lengths

•

Masking tape

•

Thin card

•

Thick plain paper

•

Newspaper and glue

•

Papier mâché pulp

•

Black and red paint

•

Tracing paper

•

Stencil paper and brush

•

Thick yellow paint

•

Varnish

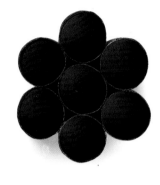

• WHAT TO DO •

1 Tape the tubes together to form a flower shape as shown. Place the flower on the thin card and draw around it. Cut out inside the line. Tape on to one end of the tubes to form a base.

2 Place the base on the thin card and draw around the flower shape again. Cut out, this time outside the line. Tape a thick paper strip along the outside of the card shape with masking tape bending into the corners. This is the lid.

3 Cover the edges of tape on both the box and the lid with torn strips of newspaper and glue.

4 With papier mâché pulp build up a ridge, sloping down to the inside, around the top of the lid.

5 Paint the inside of the lid and tubes black. When dry paint the outside red.

6 Using the template on page 98 trace and cut a stencil. Tape on to the centre of the lid and paint with thick yellow paint. Remove the stencil carefully when dry. Varnish the outside of the box to finish.

SHAKER BOX

The Shakers – a religious sect in North America now in declining numbers – were craftspeople who used natural materials and simple practical lines in their designs.

SHOPPING LIST

Corrugated cardboard

•

Tracing paper

•

Scalpel or craft knife

•

Flexible corrugated cardboard
(the kind that protects bottles)

•

Masking tape

•

Newspaper and glue

•

Paint of your choice

•

Varnish

•

5 gold paper fasteners

• WHAT TO DO •

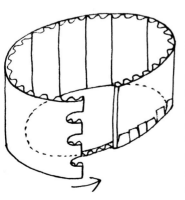

1 Trace and cut out a corrugated cardboard oval using the base template on pages 98–99. Then cut a second one 5mm/¼in larger all round.

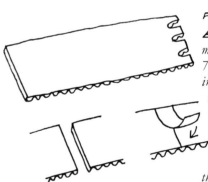

2 Cut a wide band of flexible cardboard measuring 11cm/4¼in × 71cm/28in. Cut one end into 'castellations' using the template on page 98. If necessary cut 2 pieces to make the band but join them flush with tape (on the flat side if one side is ridged).

3 Starting with the straight end at the centre of one side of the smaller oval, tape the band on the outside edge of it. Continue around the oval until complete, overlapping with the castellated edge outside. Tape the edges together on the inside.

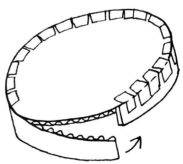

4 Cut a second band of flexible cardboard measuring 2.5cm/1in × 73cm/29½in. Tape around the outside edge of the large oval starting at the same point as the first, and overlapping as before.

ABOVE: *The Shakers made these storage boxes in all sizes and originally crafted them from natural pine and cherry.*

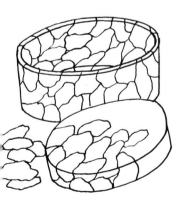

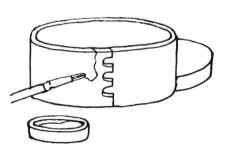

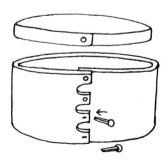

5 Cover the whole box, inside and out, with small torn pieces of glued newspaper until a smooth overall finish is achieved. Take special care when covering the castellated edge.

6 Paint the inside of the box and, when dry, paint the outside. Leave to dry.

7 Varnish. When dry make small holes and push paper fasteners through the overlaps where shown.

STAR BOX

This box is covered in mosaic pieces of shiny gold papers cut to fit into the points of the star. Sequins and foil could be added to create texture. For this box you need the kind of flexible corrugated cardboard which has a ridged side.

SHOPPING LIST

Corrugated cardboard
•
Tracing paper
•
Scalpel or craft knife
•
Flexible corrugated cardboard (the kind that protects bottles)
•
Masking tape
•
Newspaper and glue
•
Gold spray paint
•
Black paint
•
Various gold papers

• WHAT TO DO •

1 *Trace and cut a star out of the corrugated cardboard using the template on page 96. Then cut a second one 5mm/¼in larger all round.*

2 *Cut a strip of flexible cardboard measuring 2.5cm/1in x 96cm/37½in. This will form the sides of the lid. If necessary cut 2 pieces to make the strip but join them flush with tape on the flat side. Cut a second strip measuring 5cm/2in x 87cm/34in to form the sides of the box.*

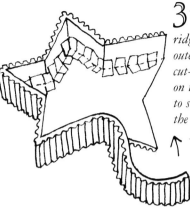

3 *Attach the wider strip of cardboard, with the ridged side outwards, to the outer edge of the smaller star cut-out with pieces of tape on the inside. Take care not to squash the ridges. Join the ends with tape inside.*
Do the same with the thinner strip and larger star cut-out.

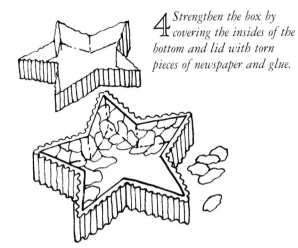

4 *Strengthen the box by covering the insides of the bottom and lid with torn pieces of newspaper and glue.*

5 *Place the 2 halves of the box, insides facing up, on some newspaper. Spray insides and sides with gold paint until well covered. Leave to dry.*

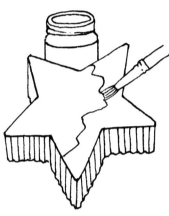

6 *Apply black paint to the bottom of the box and the top of the lid. Leave to dry.*

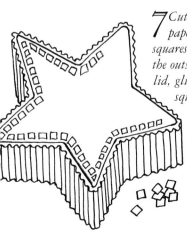

7 *Cut different gold papers into small squares. Starting at the outside edge of the lid, glue a row of squares around it, leaving gaps between to make a mosaic effect.*

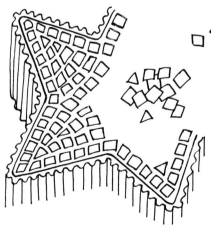

8 *Fill in with other squares, cutting different shapes to fit in the corners.*

FISH BOX

A contrast to the heavily decorated boxes, this
design is quite plain and retains its layers of torn newspaper
untouched inside. You will need the kind of flexible
corrugated cardboard which has a ridged side to it
for the sides of the box.

SHOPPING LIST

Corrugated cardboard

•

Tracing paper

•

Scalpel or craft knife

Flexible corrugated cardboard (the
kind that protects bottles)

•

Masking tape

•

Newspaper and glue

• WHAT TO DO •

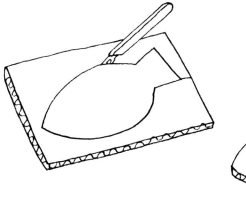

1 *Trace and cut out a corrugated
cardboard fish shape using the
template on pages 100–101. Then
cut a second one 5mm/¼in larger
all round.*

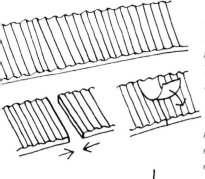

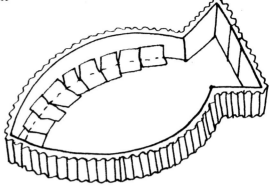

2 *Cut a wide band of flexible cardboard measuring 11cm/4¼in x 75cm/29½in. Cut this band out of 2 pieces if necessary but join them together flush with masking tape on the flat side of the cardboard.*

3 *Join the band, with the ridged side facing out, to the outside of the smaller fish shape. Use pieces of tape on the inside only. Be careful not to squash the cardboard ridges. Join the ends flush with tape on the inside.*

4 *Cut a second band of flexible cardboard measuring 2.5cm/1in x 77cm/30¼in. Tape as above to the outside of the large fish shape. Join the ends flush with tape on the inside.*

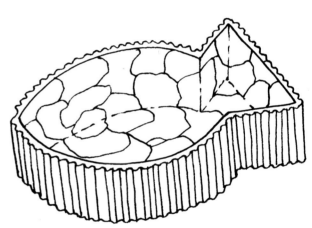

5 *Line the inside of the box and lid with pieces of torn and glued newspaper. Continue to add pieces until the box is firm and strong. Leave to dry.*

SNAKE BOX

Use the template on pages 100–101 and cut 2 snakes, one 5mm/¼in larger all round. Cut flexible corrugated cardboard into strips 4cm/1½in wide and long enough to go around the snake shapes. If the flexible cardboard has a smooth side put this on the outside. If not, cover the ridges with pieces of newspaper and glue until smooth and firm. Use red or green paint for the insides of the box, the lid and the bottom half of the box. When dry cover the outside of the lid with torn strips of patterned paper cutting the ends off level with the edge of the box.

CHRISTMAS CARD BOX

This design is a good way of recycling your most attractive Christmas cards from last year. The same idea could apply to birthday cards or postcards. You can easily make different-shaped boxes with fewer or more sides and flat lids using the same basic technique.

SHOPPING LIST

Glue
•
Old Christmas cards (same size)
•
Christmas wrapping paper
•
Green yarn
•
Thin card

• WHAT TO DO •

1 *Glue the front of 5 cards to their backs. Glue a piece of wrapping paper to the back of each and trim the edges.*

2 *Sew around the cards in blanket stitch with the yarn (see page 13). These will be the sides of the box.*

3 *Sew the cards together in a row with the pictures on the same side. Use yarn and small neat stitches between the blanket stitching. Join into a pentagon in the same way, keeping the pictures facing outwards.*

4 *Stand the pentagon on the thin card and mark the pentagon shape in pencil. Cut this out. Repeat to make a second pentagon.*

5 *Cover both sides of the pentagons with wrapping paper and trim the edges.*

ABOVE: *Ideal as a gift, the Christmas box also provides a festive way of storing small decorations after the event.*

6 *Sew around the 2 pentagon shapes in blanket stitch using the green yarn.*

7 *Join one pentagon to the bottom of the cards with yarn and small neat stitches between the blanket stitching. This is the base of the box.*

8 *Cut 5 equilateral triangles out of Christmas cards, making the sides the same length as the tops of the 5 cards. Glue each front to its back as before.*

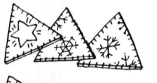

9 *Sew around each triangle in blanket stitch and yarn.*

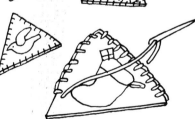

10 *Sew the triangles together to form a shallow cone shape, keeping the pictures facing outwards.*

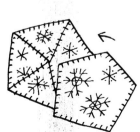

11 *Join the second pentagon to the bottom of the cone with small neat stitches.*

12 *Finally attach the lid to the top of one of the 5 cards on the bottom of the box, using yarn and neat stitches.*

CHEST OF DRAWERS

All children would love this miniature chest of drawers
to keep tiny bits and pieces in. It could also be used for small
items such as hairbands and ribbons. Try designing other items
of furniture according to the boxes you have available.

SHOPPING LIST

6 large matchboxes (or similar)
•
Glue
•
Yellow paint
•
Stiff paper/thin card
•
Cardboard tube (about
4cm/1½in in diameter)
•
Masking tape
•
Thin yellow yarn or string
•
6 beads
•
Tracing paper
•
Scalpel or craft knife
•
Silver foil or paper

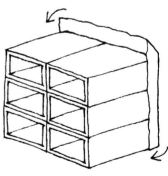

• WHAT TO DO •

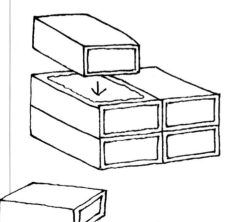

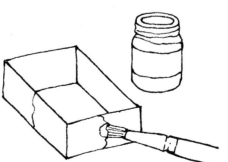

1 *Remove any card dividers from
inside the matchboxes. Glue the
boxes together to form a solid
block as shown.*

2 *Remove the 'drawers' from
the boxes. Paint one end and
half-way down the sides in yellow.
Leave to dry.*

3 *On the stiff paper or card,
mark a rectangle about
2cm/¾in wider than the
drawer block on each side.
Place over the back of the
block, folding and gluing the
overlaps to the sides.*

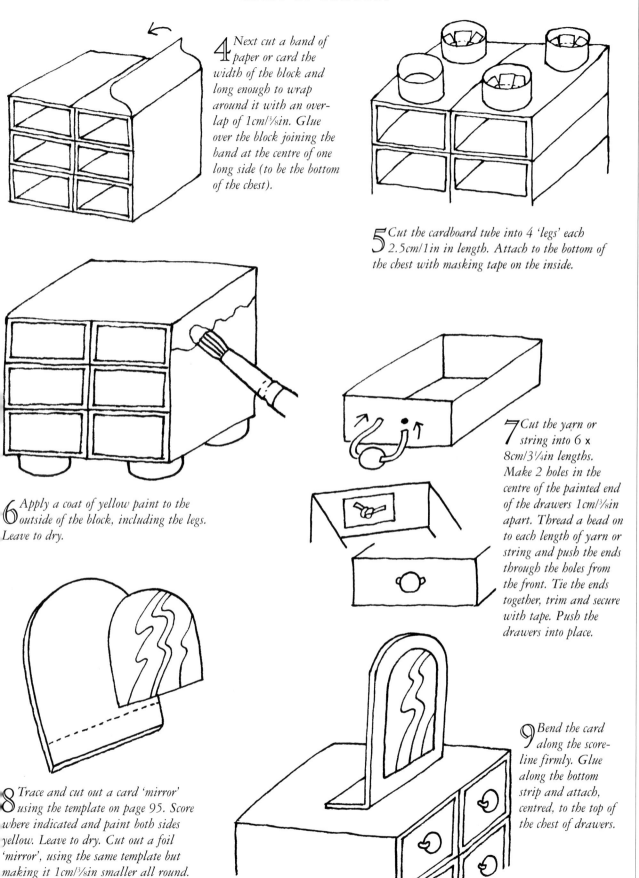

4 Next cut a band of paper or card the width of the block and long enough to wrap around it with an overlap of 1cm/⅜in. Glue over the block joining the band at the centre of one long side (to be the bottom of the chest).

5 Cut the cardboard tube into 4 'legs' each 2.5cm/1in in length. Attach to the bottom of the chest with masking tape on the inside.

6 Apply a coat of yellow paint to the outside of the block, including the legs. Leave to dry.

7 Cut the yarn or string into 6 x 8cm/3¼in lengths. Make 2 holes in the centre of the painted end of the drawers 1cm/⅜in apart. Thread a bead on to each length of yarn or string and push the ends through the holes from the front. Tie the ends together, trim and secure with tape. Push the drawers into place.

8 Trace and cut out a card 'mirror' using the template on page 95. Score where indicated and paint both sides yellow. Leave to dry. Cut out a foil 'mirror', using the same template but making it 1cm/⅜in smaller all round. Glue in position.

9 Bend the card along the scoreline firmly. Glue along the bottom strip and attach, centred, to the top of the chest of drawers.

LIDS AND INSIDES

I N ADDITION TO THE IDEAS shown so far for making and shaping boxes, there are so many different ways of creating something original or special from ready-made boxes. You can design your own decorative handles or knobs, for example, reshape the lids into different styles and divide up the insides into various compartments for storing small items.

The following pages are packed with step-by-step instructions and examples which use many of the basic techniques already covered earlier in the book and introduce some new ones. But, as always, let your imagination go to work and feel free to do your own thing according to the materials you have available and the purpose of your box.

— • DECORATING LIDS • —

Cardboard cut-outs painted and stuck on to the top of a lid
can transform a simple box into an unusual container. A template
for this example is given on page 102, but you could also use some
of the others provided at the end of the book to make fun
decorations in the same way.

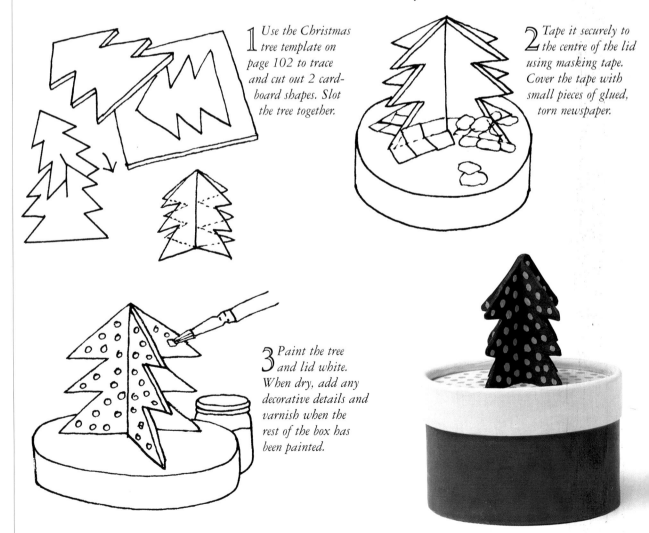

1 Use the Christmas tree template on page 102 to trace and cut out 2 cardboard shapes. Slot the tree together.

2 Tape it securely to the centre of the lid using masking tape. Cover the tape with small pieces of glued, torn newspaper.

3 Paint the tree and lid white. When dry, add any decorative details and varnish when the rest of the box has been painted.

• MAKING COMPARTMENTS •

Extend the decoration of your box to the inside.
Compartments are useful for keeping small items separate
from each other. The colouring for the inside can match
or contrast with the outside of the box.

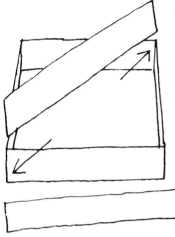

1 *Cut 2 strips of thin card to fit across the inside of the box from corner to corner, making them slightly narrower than the depth of the box.*

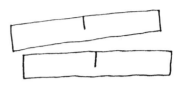

2 *Make a cut half-way down the strips of card, half-way along their length. Place in the box, slotting them together to form a cross.*

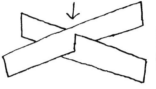

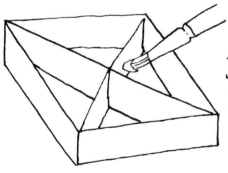

3 *Paint the different sections in bright colours, taking care not to move the card strips.*

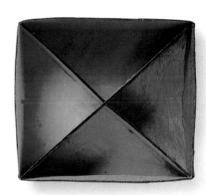

VARIATIONS

A semi-circular cheese box can be simply and neatly divided into 3 sections using 2 strips of card.

This circular box is divided with card 'teardrop' shapes placed together to form a flower.

Try making several square compartments using the same method as outlined above.

• MAKING LIDS •

The same box can be given three completely different looks by
shaping and covering the lid in various ways. Cover the bottom halves
of the boxes with paper or paint to complement the lids. Use strong
colours to emphasize the patterned edge of the lids.

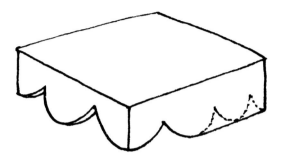

*1 Start by drawing a scalloped edge around the
sides of the lid (with one scallop at each corner).
Then cut along the marked edge with scissors.*

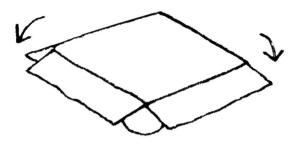

*2 Cover the lid with a piece of felt, gluing it down
neatly and trimming off the sides so that they
are level with the scalloped edges.*

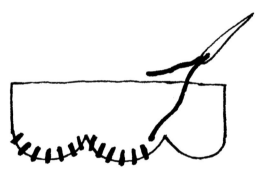

*3 Following the instructions outlined on page 13,
overstitch the scallops with black yarn or yarn
in a colour which contrasts with the felt.*

VARIATIONS

*Cut the sides of the box lid into points
(with one point at each corner). Cover
the top and then sides of the lid with
coloured corrugated cardboard.*

*Cover the lid with brown paper. Then tear
along the edges so that the white card
underneath is revealed.*

• FANCY KNOBS •

These bold little figures, set on the lids of boxes, look very
attractive. Experiment with other shapes such as flowers, insects
or fish. (See the animal templates on page 90 for ideas.)

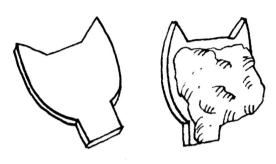

1 *Using the template on page 102 as a
base, build up the head on both sides with
papier mâché pulp.*

2 *When it's dry, tape the papier mâché head on
to the lid of the box with masking tape, making
sure that it is secure.*

3 *Cover the masking tape with small pieces of torn,
glued newspaper. Leave to dry, then paint in your
chosen colour; varnish.*

VARIATION

*A bird shape can be formed out
of papier mâché pulp, building
up a stout column for legs. To
finish, paint pointy toes on
the lid of the box.*

SECRET BOXES

*These are secret boxes in the sense
that you would not know that they were
anything more than unusual ornaments
when you first looked at them. But all of
them, from the dinosaur to the skyscraper,
have at least one storage compartment in
which to keep things. Many of the techniques
outlined earlier in the book are used in
making them and, as always, they will
inspire many original ideas.*

DUCK ON POND BOX

This really is a surprise box complete with its own tray which can be used to sort out the contents – perhaps beads or buttons. Stringing a necklace or bracelet will be much easier with this by your side or on your lap.

SHOPPING LIST

Corrugated cardboard
•
Scalpel or craft knife
•
Newspaper and glue
•
Thin card
•
Masking tape
•
Tracing paper
•
White, blue and green paint and colours of your choice
•
Green paper
•
2 pearl-headed pins
•
Varnish

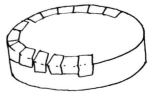

• WHAT TO DO •

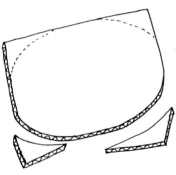

1 *Start with the pond. Cut out a piece of cardboard about 28cm/11in square and cut off the corners to create an uneven oval shape.*

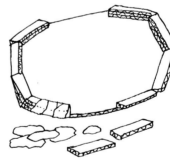

2 *Cut more cardboard into 1.5cm/⅝in wide strips and glue them on to the edge of the cardboard base building up to a height of 2cm/¼in and leaving a gap of about 10cm/4in for the duck. Cover the strips in pieces of glued newspaper.*

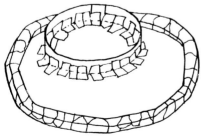

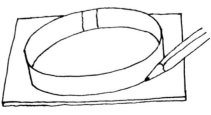

3 *Cut a strip of thin card 40cm/16in x 3cm/1¼in. Bend it to form an oval and tape the ends together, overlapping by 2.5cm/1in. Place on the cardboard, fitting into the gap, and tape firmly. Fill any holes with glued newspaper.*

4 *Cut a second strip of thin card 42.5cm/ 16¾in x 2cm/¼in. Bend it to form an oval and tape the ends together, overlapping by 2.5cm/1in. Place on some more thin card and mark around the outside. Cut out and tape this oval to the card ring to make the lid.*

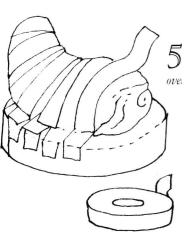

5 Crumple up some newspaper and tape on top of the lid in the form of a duck. Tape all over to achieve a solid firm shape.

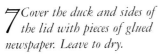

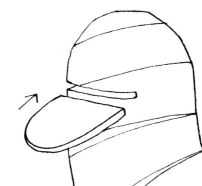

6 Trace and cut a beak out of card using the template on page 102. Make a slit in the duck's head and push in the straight edge of the beak. Tape in position.

7 Cover the duck and sides of the lid with pieces of glued newspaper. Leave to dry.

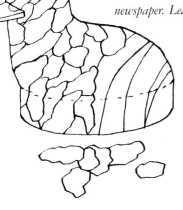

8 Paint the duck box and tray white and leave to dry. Then paint the tray blue and green giving a textured finish.

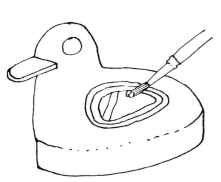

9 Now paint the beak, eyes and wings of the duck with colours of your choice, using a small paintbrush.

10 Cut the green paper into 10 pointed strips and glue them to either side of the tray inside the rim. Push the pearl-headed pins into the centre of the duck's eyes. Then varnish the box.

SKYSCRAPER BOX

This basic building principle can also be applied to create other structures. See what the boxes you've collected suggest to you – perhaps a clock tower (add a clock face to the four sides) or a lighthouse (using different sized tubes)?

SHOPPING LIST

6 boxes ranging from large to
small (with lids)

•

Scalpel or craft knife

•

Newspaper and glue

•

Thick card (about 5mm/¼in thick)
or layers of card this thickness

•

White and yellow (or gold) paint

•

Silver foil or paper

•

Double-sided tape

•

Small stick or straw

• WHAT TO DO •

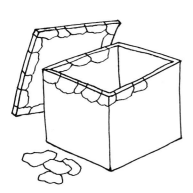

1 *Prepare the boxes starting with the largest one. Cut off the top carefully and neaten any cut edges with pieces of glued newspaper.*

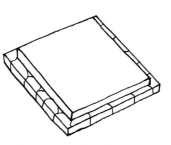

2 *Cut a piece of card 5mm/¼in smaller than the top of the box and glue it to one side. Card side down, this will be both the lid of the largest box and the bottom of the next one above it.*

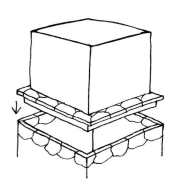

3 *Glue the bottom of the next largest box on to the top of this lid (not the side with the card).*

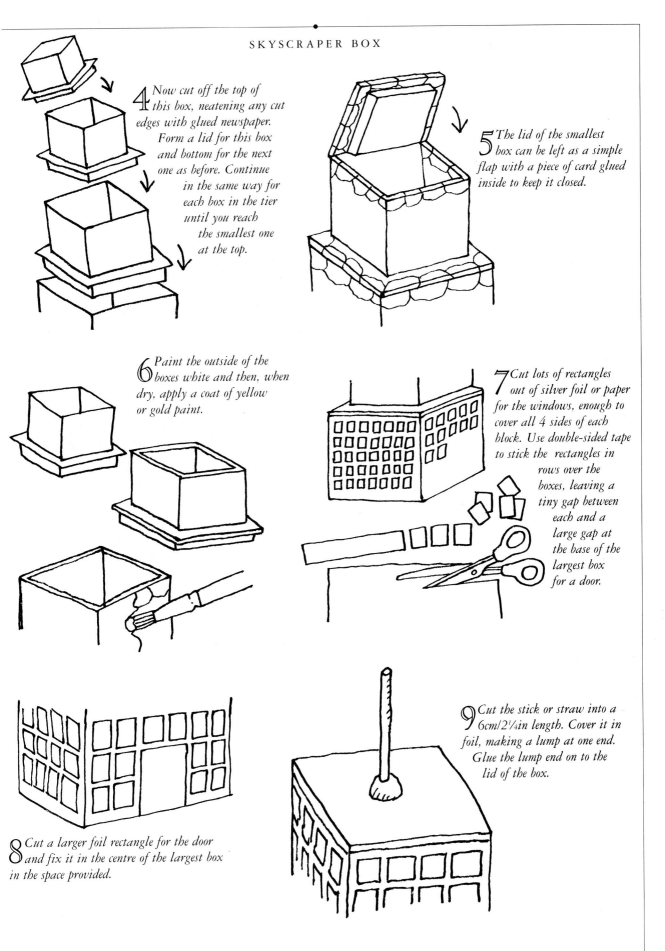

4 Now cut off the top of this box, neatening any cut edges with glued newspaper. Form a lid for this box and bottom for the next one as before. Continue in the same way for each box in the tier until you reach the smallest one at the top.

5 The lid of the smallest box can be left as a simple flap with a piece of card glued inside to keep it closed.

6 Paint the outside of the boxes white and then, when dry, apply a coat of yellow or gold paint.

7 Cut lots of rectangles out of silver foil or paper for the windows, enough to cover all 4 sides of each block. Use double-sided tape to stick the rectangles in rows over the boxes, leaving a tiny gap between each and a large gap at the base of the largest box for a door.

8 Cut a larger foil rectangle for the door and fix it in the centre of the largest box in the space provided.

9 Cut the stick or straw into a 6cm/2¼in length. Cover it in foil, making a lump at one end. Glue the lump end on to the lid of the box.

DINOSAUR BOX

This large, brightly coloured dinosaur would look terrific in any child's room – and provide a useful home for smaller relatives!

SHOPPING LIST

Shoe box with removable lid

•

2 cardboard tubes 23cm/9in long x 4cm/1½in in diameter

•

Scalpel or craft knife

•

Masking tape

•

Thin card

•

Newspaper and glue

•

Corrugated cardboard

•

4 cardboard tubes 10cm/4in long x 4cm/1½in in diameter

•

Paint in white, orange and assorted colours

•

Varnish

• WHAT TO DO •

1 *Measure and mark the mid-point of each end of the box. Draw around each of the long cardboard tubes in the centre of each of these ends. Carefully cut out the circles inside the lines to make 2 holes.*

2 *Cut a fringe of card 1cm/⅜in deep at the end of one tube. On the other cut a fringe 1cm/⅜in deep, lengthening to 2cm/¾in for half the circle. Push a tube through each hole with the fringed end inside the box (and the longer part of the fringe uppermost for the second 'neck' tube). Push the fringes back and tape inside the box. Tape pieces of thin card over the holes.*

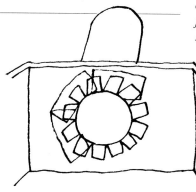

3 *Crush some newspaper into a ball. Push it slightly into the 'neck' tube and tape it securely at the end. Tape a pointed ball of newspaper on to the end of the 'tail'.*

4 *Cut 4 circles of cardboard 4cm/1½in in diameter. Cut some jagged claws on one side and tape to each of the shorter tubes so that the claws point forwards. Make 4 balls of crushed newspaper and stick one securely to the top of each tube. Tape on to the sides of the box.*

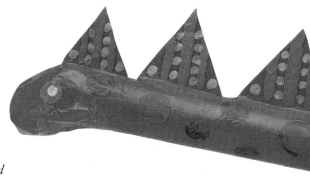

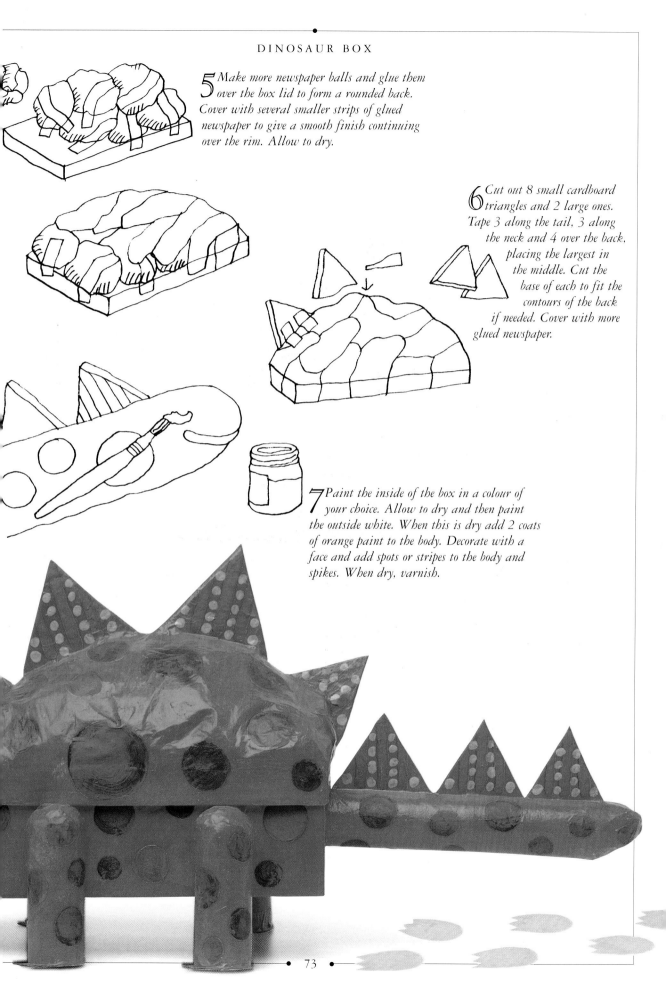

5 Make more newspaper balls and glue them over the box lid to form a rounded back. Cover with several smaller strips of glued newspaper to give a smooth finish continuing over the rim. Allow to dry.

6 Cut out 8 small cardboard triangles and 2 large ones. Tape 3 along the tail, 3 along the neck and 4 over the back, placing the largest in the middle. Cut the base of each to fit the contours of the back if needed. Cover with more glued newspaper.

7 Paint the inside of the box in a colour of your choice. Allow to dry and then paint the outside white. When this is dry add 2 coats of orange paint to the body. Decorate with a face and add spots or stripes to the body and spikes. When dry, varnish.

FAMILY GROUP BOX

This can easily be adapted according to the tubes you have available and the number of people you want to include in the group. Make your own family or gathering of friends. A wedding group would make a wonderful present.

SHOPPING LIST

3 different width tubes

•

Scalpel or craft knife

•

Newspaper and glue

•

Masking tape

•

Thick card

•

Papier mâché pulp

•

Black and white paint

•

Bright paints of your choice

•

Varnish

• WHAT TO DO •

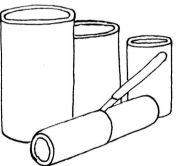

1 *Cut the widest tube into lengths of 20cm/8in and 18cm/7in, the medium one into a length of 15cm/6in and the smallest tube into 2 lengths of 10cm/4in.*

2 *Screw newspaper into balls, one for each tube, and each wider than the tube it will match. Place each ball on a piece of newspaper. Wrap up and twist the base into a 'stalk' about 4cm/1½in long. Tape together securely.*

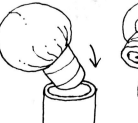

3 *Fold pieces of newspaper into 4cm/1½in wide strips and roll around each stalk until it fits snugly into its tube. Tape around the stalk until it is firm and neat.*

4 Place the heads in the tubes and arrange in a close group making sure you can remove each head without knocking off any of the others! Tape the tubes on to a rectangle of thick card.

5 Stick layers of papier mâché pulp around the base of the tubes to form the feet and skirts.

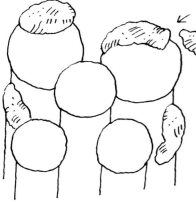

6 Add other details in papier mâché pulp such as hair, hats and arms. Leave to dry.

7 Cut card triangles for noses and half circles for ears. Cut slits in the heads with a scalpel or craft knife and push into position. Secure with tape. Paint the heads white.

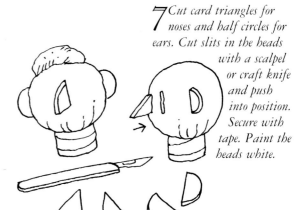

8 Paint the insides of the tubes with black paint and the outsides with white. Leave to dry.

9 Paint the figures in bright colours, adding details when the base colours are dry. Paint the card base black.

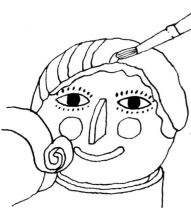

10 When all the paint is completely dry add a coat of varnish all over the box to give a durable finish.

VAN BOX

This basic vehicle can be turned into an ambulance,
army truck (painted in camouflage colours) or police van. Use
coloured bottle-tops stuck on the roof to make the lights.

SHOPPING LIST

2 cardboard boxes (1 large,
1 small)

•

Masking tape

•

Newspaper and glue

•

Corrugated cardboard

•

Black paint

•

Green shiny paper or
green paint

•

Black paper

•

Silver foil

•

2 paper fasteners

•

Thread

•

2 colourful pictures

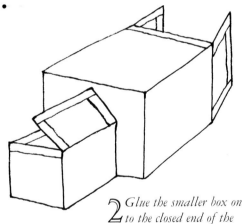

• WHAT TO DO •

1 *Prepare the boxes to
give the large one
'doors' at the back and
the smaller one a flap
opening on top. Tape
along all cut edges.*

2 *Glue the smaller box on
to the closed end of the
large one, centred and flush
with the bottom.*

3 *Cut 12 cardboard circles
5cm/2in in diameter. Glue 3
together for each of the 4 wheels.
Cover in pieces of glued newspaper.
Paint black and leave to dry.
Paint the insides of the boxes
black and leave to dry.*

ABOVE: *Decorate your van in any way you like and glue
your own pictures or drawings on to the sides.*

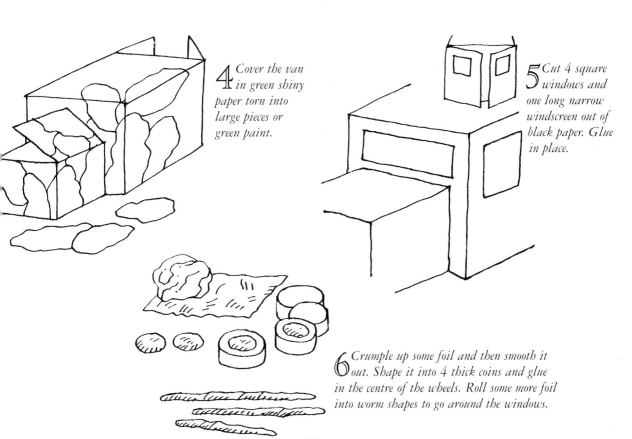

4 Cover the van in green shiny paper torn into large pieces or green paint.

5 Cut 4 square windows and one long narrow windscreen out of black paper. Glue in place.

6 Crumple up some foil and then smooth it out. Shape it into 4 thick coins and glue in the centre of the wheels. Roll some more foil into worm shapes to go around the windows.

7 *Glue worm shapes around the windows to form the frames, then glue the wheels into position.*

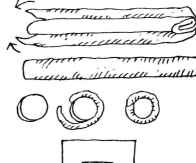

8 *Make a front bumper by gluing foil around a strip of folded newspaper a little longer than the front of the van and sticking in place. Cut a piece of foil for a radiator and make 2 headlights out of small circles of black-painted cardboard edged in rolled foil. Glue in position above the bumper.*

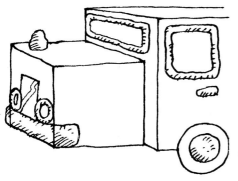

9 *Make the 2 door handles and hood decoration out of foil and stick in place.*

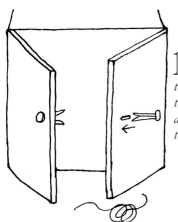

10 *Push the 2 paper fasteners through the back doors and bend the ends back inside. Wind a length of thread around them to close the doors.*

11 *To decorate glue colourful pictures cut out from magazines or patterned paper, on to the sides and roof of the van. Leave to dry.*

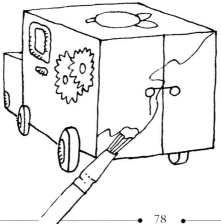

12 *Varnish the windows, headlights and wheels. If painted, varnish the exterior as well to give a durable finish.*

BASKET OF FRUIT

Unopened, this splendid basket would make an unusual centrepiece
for a feast or celebration – even more so if it was painted in gold and silver
and dusted with glue and glitter. Crumple up foil instead of raffia to
complete the dazzling effect.

SHOPPING LIST

Newspaper and glue

•

Masking tape

•

Bright paints of your choice,
including yellow and white

•

Tracing paper

•

Green and dark brown paper

•

Black pen

•

Scalpel or craft knife

•

2 x 5cm/2in thin wooden sticks

•

Shoe box with removable lid

•

Varnish

•

Raffia

•

Thin card

• WHAT TO DO •

1 Screw up some news-
paper into life-size
fruit shapes and secure
them with tape. Make
1 pineapple, 1 pear,
1 orange, 2 apples,
1 lemon, 2 bananas,
2 strawberries and
3 cherries.

2 Cover the news-
paper fruits with
torn pieces of glued
newspaper until the
shapes are complete.
Finish with small
pieces of paper
to achieve a
smoothish surface.
Leave to dry.

3 Paint the fruits in
bright colours. Two
coats may be necessary.
Add details when dry
with a small brush.

4 Using the tem-
plates on pages
102–103, trace
and cut leaves for
the pineapple,
strawberries, 1
apple and the pear
in green paper.
Draw on veins
with a black pen.

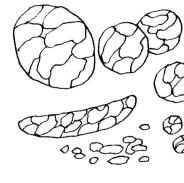

ABOVE: *You can combine any fruits you wish in this basket —
mangos and papayas would give a more exotic result.*

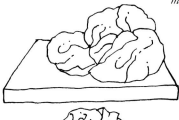

*5 Cover the lid of the
box with glued
scrunched-up newspaper.*

*6 Make a small
incision in the top of
the pear, pineapple and
1 apple and glue the end
of the leaves in position.
Glue leaves on top of the
strawberries. Add the 2
wooden sticks next to the
apple and pear leaves.*

*7 Place the fruits in position on top of
the paper and stick together with more
gluey paper. Trickle glue into any gaps to
hold the fruits in place. Leave to dry.*

8 *Varnish the fruits (they may need 2 coats).*

9 *Cut the raffia into smallish lengths and scrunch them up. Poke in between the fruits to cover all the newspaper.*

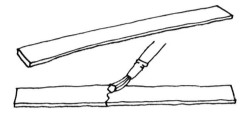

10 *Cut the card into a 62cm/24½in x 3cm/1¼in strip and paint both sides yellow. This will be the handle.*

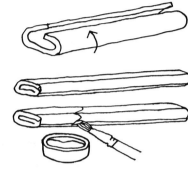

11 *Fold some newspaper into a strip 3–5cm/1¼–2in wide and long enough to go around the sides of the box lid. Tape the strip together, then paint it white and, when dry, yellow.*

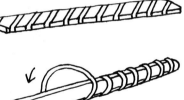

12 *When the handle and newspaper strip are dry, decorate both with narrow strips of dark brown paper, winding it around them.*

13 *Stick the ends of the handle on to each side of the lid. Glue the newspaper strip around the edge of the lid covering the ends of the handle.*

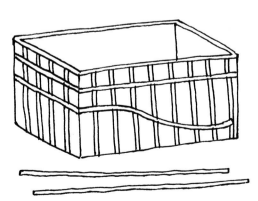

14 *Paint the main box yellow. When dry decorate with more narrow strips of dark brown paper, sticking them on in a checked pattern.*

15 *Varnish the handle, the edge of the lid and the main box. Leave to dry.*

SNOWY VILLAGE BOX

A very pretty jewellery box which would enhance any bedroom. All kinds of variations on this theme are possible – just let the boxes you have at hand inspire you. To make chimneys just cut small pieces of card, fold to shape and attach with masking tape.

SHOPPING LIST

Thin card

•

Shoe box with removable lid

•

5 small boxes

•

Tracing paper

•

Scalpel or craft knife

•

Thick card or corrugated cardboard

•

Masking tape

•

Newspaper and glue

•

Papier mâché pulp (see page 12)

•

White paint and assorted colours

•

Varnish

• WHAT TO DO •

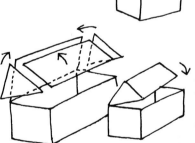

1 *Cut a strip of thin card long enough to go around the lid of the shoe box and at least twice the depth of the lid edge. Cut one long edge into a gentle wave. Cut into 4 to fit the lid sides and glue on. Adjust the ends to meet.*

2 *Make the small boxes into houses with different lid 'roofs' – some removable, some hinged (see the Jewelled Casket on pages 38–39) and some with card chimneys.*

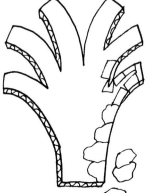

3 *Trace and cut out a tree shape from the thick card or corrugated cardboard using the template on page 103. If using corrugated cardboard, cover the edges with masking tape and strips of glued newspaper.*

4 *Glue the houses in place on the box lid. Tape the tree in front. Build up papier mâché snowdrifts around the bases of the houses, tree and one roof. Leave to dry.*

LEFT: *Keep larger items of jewellery inside the bottom of the box and smaller, more precious, items in the little 'houses' on top. Hang rings on the tree!*

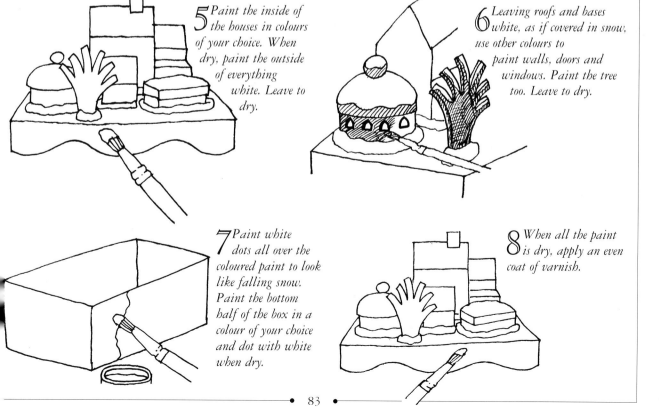

5 *Paint the inside of the houses in colours of your choice. When dry, paint the outside of everything white. Leave to dry.*

6 *Leaving roofs and bases white, as if covered in snow, use other colours to paint walls, doors and windows. Paint the tree too. Leave to dry.*

7 *Paint white dots all over the coloured paint to look like falling snow. Paint the bottom half of the box in a colour of your choice and dot with white when dry.*

8 *When all the paint is dry, apply an even coat of varnish.*

HAT BOX

You can transform any box into something attractive and special by covering it with material. Tea-dyed fabrics (see the instructions on page 13) are most attractive and give a mellow antique look. This box looks good enough to wear and, left lying on a side table or chair, will fool everyone.

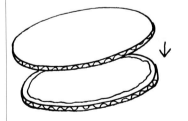

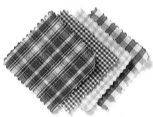

SHOPPING LIST

Corrugated cardboard	Fabric glue
Scalpel or craft knife	Pinking shears
Newspaper and glue	Striped fabric for the hat band (60cm/23½ in x 7cm/2¾in)
Thick card	Thin grey yarn
Masking tape	Red and black checked fabric
White paint	Wadding (batting) or stuffing
Yellow checked fabric to cover the hat (75cm/29½in)	Beige thread

• WHAT TO DO •

1 Make the hat out of cardboard first. Draw 2 circles 28cm/11in in diameter on the corrugated cardboard and cut out. Glue together.

2 *Cut a strip of thick card 50cm/19½in x 8cm/3¼in and bend it to form a ring. Tape it together overlapping by 1cm/⅜in. Place it in the centre of the cardboard circles and tape in position. This will be the base of the box.*

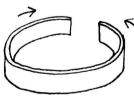

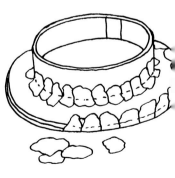

3 *Cover the tape with glued pieces of newspaper until firm, then paper over the edges of the cardboard. Leave to dry and paint the inside white.*

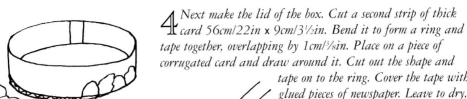

4 Next make the lid of the box. Cut a second strip of thick card 56cm/22in x 9cm/3½in. Bend it to form a ring and tape together, overlapping by 1cm/⅜in. Place on a piece of corrugated card and draw around it. Cut out the shape and tape on to the ring. Cover the tape with glued pieces of newspaper. Leave to dry, then paint the inside white.

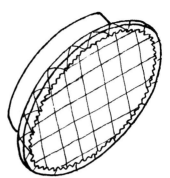

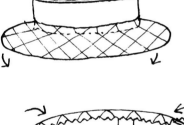

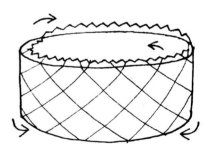

5 Next cover the hat with fabric. Cut a ring of yellow checked fabric to cover the brim of the hat adding 3cm/1¼in to the inner and outer edges. Place the ring on to the glued brim smoothing it down in position. Glue the edges underneath.

6 Using pinking shears, cut a circle of yellow fabric 27cm/10½in in diameter. Glue into position.

7 Using pinking shears, cut a strip of yellow fabric 10cm/4in x 50cm/19½in. Glue it on flush with the rim. Glue the overlap carefully inside the top.

8 Next cover the lid. Using pinking shears, cut another strip of yellow fabric 12cm/4¾in x 56cm/22in. Glue in place, pressing the overlaps down.

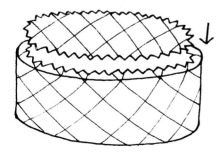

9 Using pinking shears, cut a circle of yellow fabric 16cm/6¼in in diameter. Glue in place, smoothing down carefully.

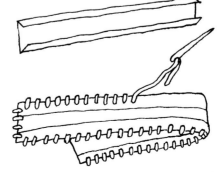

10 Next make the hat band. Fold the long edges of the striped fabric in by about 1cm/⅜in and, using yarn, overstitch along both edges and one end (see page 13).

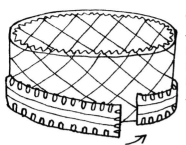

11 *Glue this band around the lid of the hat, flush with the bottom. Overlap the ends so that the stitched end is on top.*

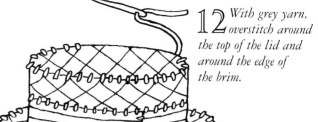

12 *With grey yarn, overstitch around the top of the lid and around the edge of the brim.*

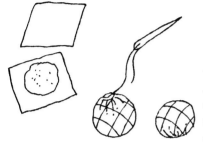

13 *Next make the flowers. Cut 4 5cm/2in squares of black checked fabric. Place a little stuffing or wadding (batting) in the centre of each. Make a row of running stitches around the outside of the squares using a needle and thread and draw the material together to form a ball.*

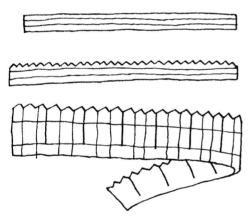

14 *Cut the red checked fabric into 4 20cm/8in x 6cm/2¼in strips, cutting along one edge with pinking shears. Make a fringe along the pinked edge by cutting into every third point to within 2 cm/¾in of the straight edge using ordinary scissors.*

15 *Holding the straight edge of each strip against the back of a ball, stitch in place, winding the strip around the ball until complete. Make 4 flowers in all.*

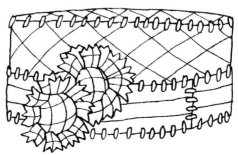

16 *Finish by sewing the flowers on to one side of the lid of the hat, grouping them near the base.*

TEMPLATES

*The following pages contain all
the templates you need for the projects
in this book. Overleaf is a list of the
templates required for each one. To
use them you need tracing paper and
a pencil. You can enlarge or reduce the
templates on a photocopier if your box
is a different size to the ones used in the
projects. To cut a template out of card
or cardboard use a scalpel or craft knife.
For cutting one from fabric you need
sharp scissors and pins. See page 12
for full step-by-step instructions
on Using a Template.*

Index of templates in alphabetical order

TEA-TIME BOX
Teapot

TEA-TIME BOX
Leaf

TEA-TIME BOX
Cup and saucer

TEA-TIME BOX
Leaf

TEA-TIME BOX
Cake

THREAD
REEL BOX

BIRD BOX

ANIMALS VARIATION
Rabbit

ANIMALS VARIATION
Fish

LIZARD BOX

TORN PAPER BOX

ANIMALS VARIATION
Dog

ANIMALS VARIATION
Cat

APPLIQUÉ LETTERS BOX
Heart

APPLIQUÉ
LETTERS BOX
Bird Wing

APPLIQUÉ LETTERS BOX
Bird Body

ROOSTER BOX

STRING BOX
Teacup

STRING BOX
Eggcup

STRING BOX
Crown

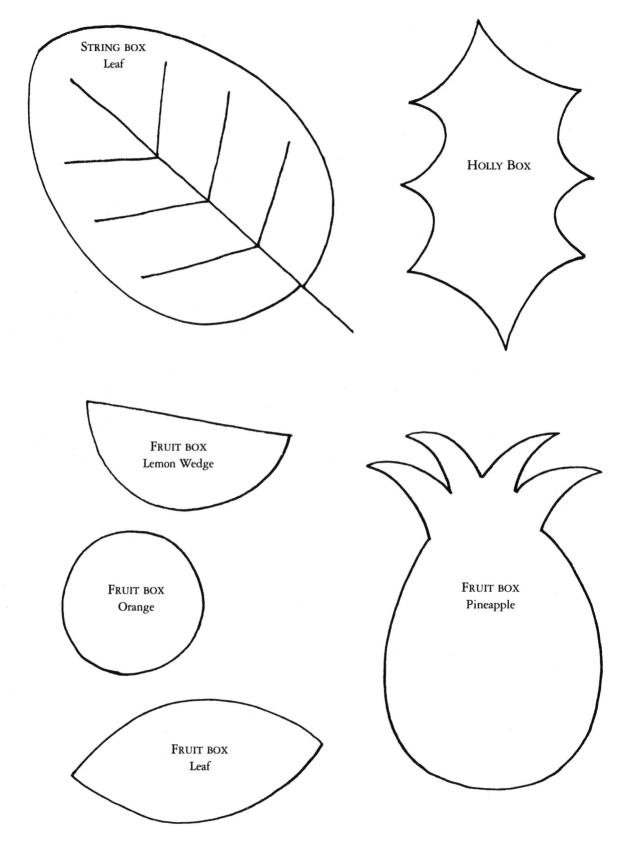

STRING BOX
Leaf

HOLLY BOX

FRUIT BOX
Lemon Wedge

FRUIT BOX
Orange

FRUIT BOX
Pineapple

FRUIT BOX
Leaf

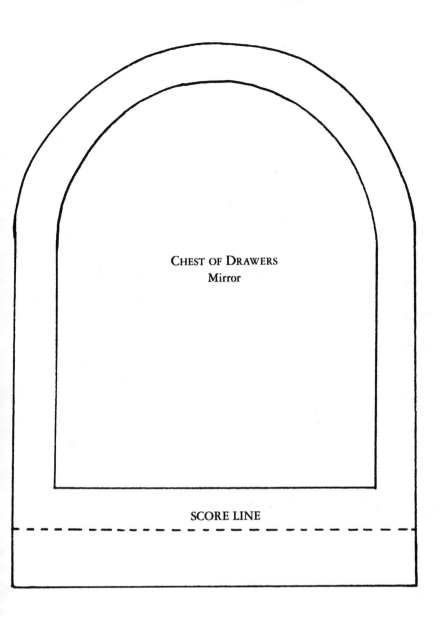

CHEST OF DRAWERS
Mirror

SCORE LINE

LATTICE BOX
Shape 1

LATTICE BOX
Shape 2

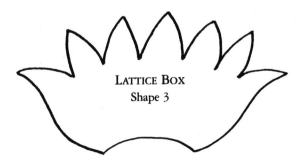

LATTICE BOX
Shape 3

LATTICE
BOX
Shape 4

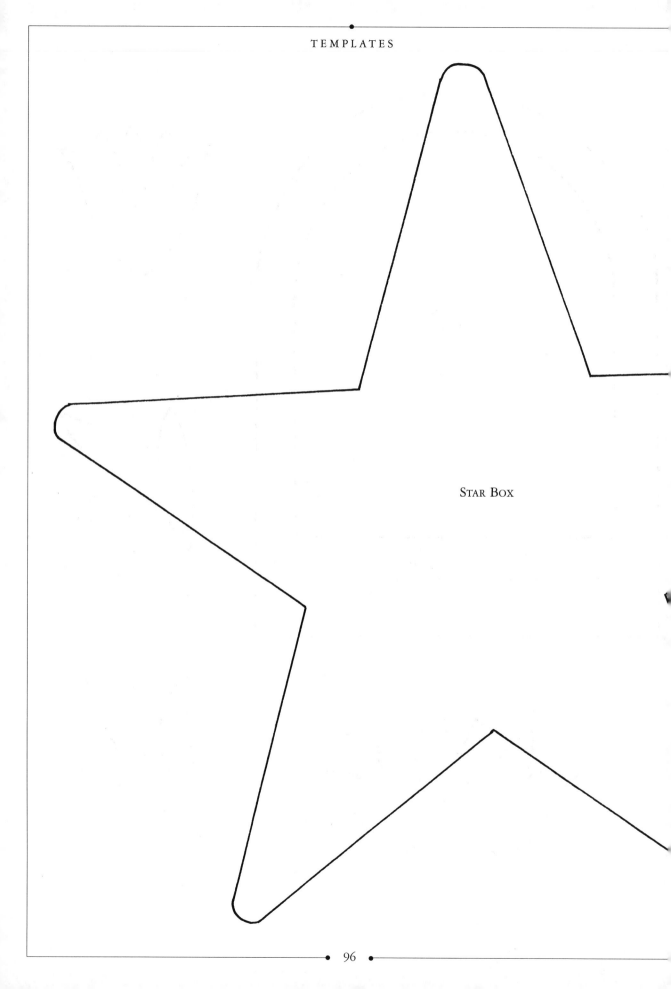

STAR BOX

DICE BOX

DESK TIDY

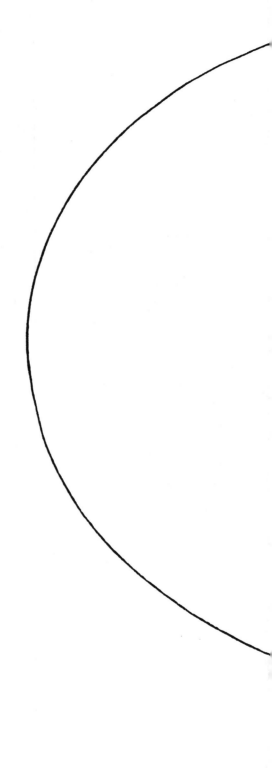

SHAKER BOX
Castellated Edge

SHAKER BOX
Base

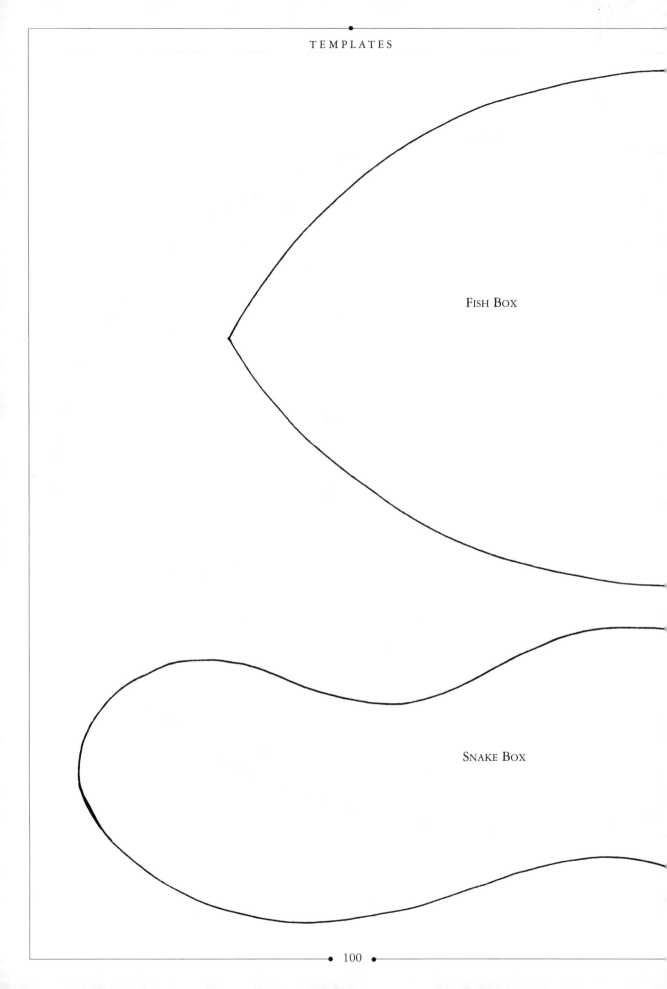

FISH BOX

SNAKE BOX

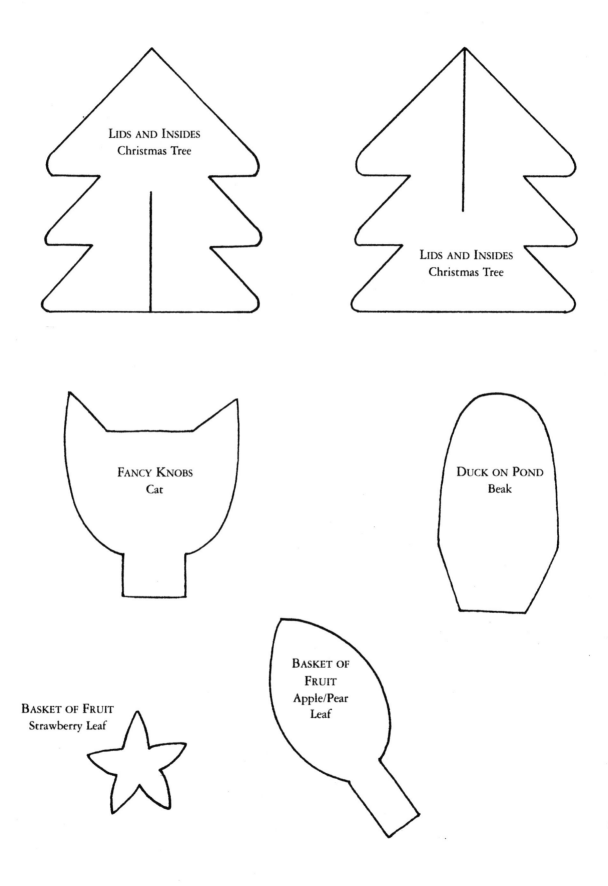

LIDS AND INSIDES
Christmas Tree

LIDS AND INSIDES
Christmas Tree

FANCY KNOBS
Cat

DUCK ON POND
Beak

BASKET OF
FRUIT
Apple/Pear
Leaf

BASKET OF FRUIT
Strawberry Leaf

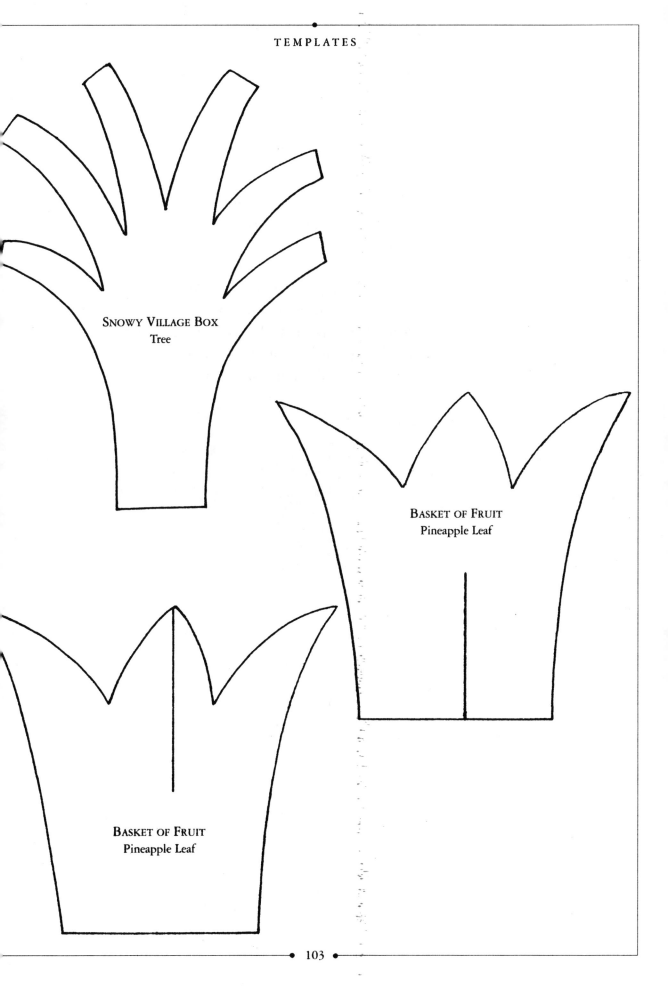

SNOWY VILLAGE BOX
Tree

BASKET OF FRUIT
Pineapple Leaf

BASKET OF FRUIT
Pineapple Leaf

ACKNOWLEDGEMENTS

Clare Beaton would like to thank the
following for their hard work in helping
to create this book: Geoff Dann for his
inspirational photography; Gavin Weightman
for typing the original manuscript; DTP
designer Claire Graham and Senior Art
Editor Ruth Hope for designing the book.
Also many thanks to Susan Martineau for
her superb copy-editing, and to Catherine
Ward for her editorial assistance.